MY
radiant
CANDLE

MW00833905

MY
radiant
CANDLE

one woman's incredible journey of
faith, spirit, courage, & love

ROD T. ELLIS

TATE PUBLISHING & *Enterprises*

My Radiant Candle
Copyright © 2008 by Rod T. Ellis. All rights reserved.

No part of this publication may be reproduced, stored in a retrieval system or transmitted in any way by any means, electronic, mechanical, photocopy, recording or otherwise without the prior permission of the author except as provided by USA copyright law.

All Scriptures are taken from the *Holy Bible, New International Version* ®, Copyright © 1973, 1978, 1984 by International Bible Society. Used by permission of Zondervan Publishing House. All rights reserved.

The opinions expressed by the author are not necessarily those of Tate Publishing, LLC.

Published by Tate Publishing & Enterprises, LLC
127 E. Trade Center Terrace | Mustang, Oklahoma 73064 USA
1.888.361.9473 | www.tatepublishing.com

Tate Publishing is committed to excellence in the publishing industry. The company reflects the philosophy established by the founders, based on Psalm 68:11,
"The Lord gave the word and great was the company of those who published it."

Book design copyright © 2008 by Tate Publishing, LLC. All rights reserved.
Cover design by Janae J. Glass
Interior design by Nathan Harmony

Published in the United States of America

ISBN: 978-1-60696-652-5
1. Biography & Autobiography: Medical
2. Biography & Autobiography: Religious
08.11.06

Dedication

I'd like to dedicate this book to the memory of my late wife, Denise Ellis, and our children, Raechel and Richard. *My Radiant Candle* is a tribute to her incredible strength, courage, and faith. Denise was an incredible mother who was very devoted to her family. We were very fortunate to have her, even if for only a short time.

Acknowledgements

Special thanks to my family and friends who helped us through a difficult time in our lives with many unique challenges. To Denise's best friend, Tammy Grosskopf, an incredible friend to Denise who was always there for her from beginning to end. I don't think she ever missed a single opportunity to show her love and support for her dear friend Denise. Tammy showed everyone the meaning of a true friend.

Our church families from Trinity United Methodist Church of Gainesville, Capri Christian Church of Isle of Capri, and First Baptist Church of Naples were amazing; we could not have made it through this struggle without their never-ending support.

I would also like to thank the doctors who took a special interest in Denise and provided her with the best care known to mankind. The love and care they showed to Denise will not soon be forgotten. Dr. Friedman, Dr. Mendenhall, Dr. Rubin, Dr. Moscowicz, and their staffs will always have my utmost respect for the help they bring to those in need

TABLE OF *Contents*

Foreword

Yea, though I walk through the valley of the shadow
of death, I will fear no evil: for thou art with me; thy
rod and thy staff they comfort me.

Psalm 23:4

I came that they may have life, and have it abundantly.

John 10:10

"Abundant living in the shadow of death." That's how I would
describe Rod and Denise Ellis' life during her illness. For
anyone facing a debilitating or life threatening illness of his
or her own or a loved one, here is a real story of how to do it.
Their story is not a soppy sentimental attempt to put a positive spin on tragedy—it is a true-life account of how one can
actually find real joy, fulfillment, and peace while undergoing
the most difficult of life circumstances.

This is a story of hope, but it is also immensely practical—
with enormously valuable insight on dealing with the medical establishment including the importance and inevitable
frustrations of the patient's health advocate. For a guy who
self deprecatingly describes himself as "just a guy who makes

sandwiches for a living," Rod Ellis is a gifted storyteller. He permits the reader to enter into his mind and his heart as he and Denise confront the challenges of her disease.

This is a story of our times. As medical science has progressed, we have entered an era where many people are living long lives under the shadow of "terminal" illness. Our science is helping to keep us alive much longer—including greatly extending lifespan following receipt of a "death sentence" diagnosis from one's doctor. This fact is combining with the demographics of an aging population, resulting in a drastic increase in the number of people who, at any point in time, are coping with life in the shadow of death. It is a societal reality raising a host of important questions about many of our established values and our approach to medical science, health care and even to life itself.

This is a story of love. In a day of self centered relationships and marriages that often disintegrate at the first sign of stress or even boredom, here is a true love story of our times. Two ordinary people, both with numerous prior failed relationships, discover in the midst of acute crises a deep and abiding love for each other that bears the unbearable. The reader may profitably seek the answer between these pages to the question: From whence cometh such enduring love between such fragile mortals?

Most importantly this is a real life story of faith—the kind of faith that doesn't just ease the process of dying, but brings abundance to the process of living. This is not a story of how to die. It is a story of how to live.

Ed Garvin
Gainesville, Florida

Walking Through Fire

Cause I'm not who I was
When I took my first step
And I'm clinging to the promise
You're not through with me yet
So if all of these trials
Bring me closer to you
Then I will go through the fire
If you want me to
Ginny Owens, "If You Want Me To"[1]

We had come to Kazbor's to meet and discuss what was happening in my life, eat a few chicken wings, and quench our thirst. Ed was a very good friend, often encouraging me through some difficult happenings in life. I always appreciated his input because he had a totally different mentality than I; Ed was a thinker, and I am a feeler. Ed is a very accomplished CPA and attorney, who deals primarily in real estate. Now that's a lot of thinking. As for me, I'm the guy who always follows his heart, sometimes right and sometimes wrong; I trust that. God lives there, so I figure that's a good way to live my life. If a mistake is made by following that line of thinking or feeling, I should say, then there must be good reason for it.

Ed turned to me and asked, "So how are you doing, Rod?"

"Well, not that great, Ed," I replied. "I have a sense that there is this very large fire waiting in my path, and I have no choice but to walk through it. The fire is hot and the road through it is long. There is no way around, under, or over the fire, and I just know I'm going to be badly burned. You know, I'm just not looking forward to that." I chuckled uncomfortably and tried to swallow.

Ed responded, "Well, you know I'm here if you need me, and the Lord will be there with you all the way, Rod." Ed was being a feeler, for just a moment.

My wife, Denise, had been fighting cancer for about eight years or so. There had been as many ups as downs, but we had always found a way to keep her alive and fight the good fight. However, things had changed and corners had been turned. Denise's cancer had become more aggressive, recently diagnosed with three new brain tumors much larger that what we had dealt with in the past. On top of that, I had moved to Naples for business purposes and was trying to find the right time for the rest of the family to join me there.

Dr. Friedman spoke candidly to me and said, "This is a new ballgame, Rod; I no longer feel as though a cure is possible as I had hoped. The tumors are larger than before and coming more frequently. We've never had to do surgery in the past, and now we will have to remove these tumors."

I collected myself, looked him in the eye and asked him the question I usually avoided, "In your best estimate, what are we looking at—as far as how much time we have left?"

"We are probably looking at months, not years. It's hard to say for sure, but you are not looking at a lot of time." I shook his hand and thanked him for all he had done and told him I really appreciated his honesty. "No problem, you take care, and I'll see you later," he said as he walked away.

Early on, I had chosen the narrow path of righteousness, the path that would take me down the road I did not wish to travel. I loved my wife with all my heart, body, and soul, and I would be there for her no matter what. I'd heard stories of how some men actually leave their wives in times of sickness; I could not conceive of it. Denise gave me her heart, and I would give her mine, at any cost. Through my travels through many valleys of fighting cancer, I learned that we were definitely not alone. God had performed many unimaginable acts of mercy, love, and kindness for us, and I knew he would continue to do so. I would take Him with me wherever I went.

The thoughts of walking through a blazing fire reminds me of the story of Shadrach, Meshach, and Abednego and how their loyalty to God sent them into a blazing furnace. The book of Daniel tells the story.

> The king's command was so urgent and the furnace so hot that the flames of the fire killed the soldiers who took up Shadrach, Meshach and Abednego, and these three men, firmly tied, fell into the blazing furnace.
>
> Daniel 3:22–23

King Nebuchadnezzar had ordered that all in his kingdom worship an idol made of gold but the ones who had come to know the Lord refused. When the king gazed into the furnace, he was stunned to see four men, not three, and walking around in the fire.

> He said, "Look! I see four men walking around in the fire, unbound and unharmed, and the fourth looks like a son of the gods." Nebuchadnezzar then approached the opening of the blazing furnace and shouted, "Shadrach, Meshach and Abednego, servants of the Most High god, come out! Come here!" So Shadrach, Meshach and Abednego came out of the fire, and the satraps, prefects, governors and royal advisers crowded around them. They saw that the fire had not harmed their bodies, nor was a hair of their heads singed; their robes were not scorched, and there was no smell of fire on them.
>
> Daniel 3:25–27

The day finally came when it was time for me to venture into the fire. However, something was different about me, I was not who I had been first borne to be. My faith had grown by leaps and bounds, and I was proud to be the one who would show others how the Almighty God is there to help us walk through the fires of our lives. The song written by Jars of Clay was being etched into my mind, especially one specific line that goes like this, "Man, the trouble is we don't know who we are instead."[2]

However, I knew who I was instead, and it would make all the difference in the world. In my mind, I was a warrior, much like the man known as "Braveheart." I was here to protect the woman I loved and see her through this terrible ordeal. I had a greater cause as well, the cause of freedom.

A particular freedom that is given to us by none other than Jesus Christ himself. A freedom that all men had a right to but perhaps for different reasons, their freedom was being unfairly denied to them. And so, I braced myself and steadily walked into the fire.

God sent his armies, however, not to rescue me but to help me; the fire had to be endured. Angels would come, give me rest, and put salve on my wounds. Soldiers would arrive at just the right moment and carry me on their backs to keep me moving forward. Trees would fall in front of me, providing a bridge to cross over the hot lava that was sometimes oozing in front of me. And Denise was there with me all the while, encouraging me to keep moving forward, encouraging me as she had done so many times before. And one day, we emerged from the flames, and we came to a meadow. By this time, Denise was walking way ahead of me, but I could see her in the distance. There, to my amazement and delight stood our Lord Jesus with his arms wrapped tightly around Denise in a loving embrace. They were both wearing white robes and the clouds formed like welcoming hands surrounded them as a beautiful rainbow formed and a white dove ascended into the sky. Denise had made it safely home, and I had to return to my family, my friends, and my children.

Unfortunately, I was not unscathed like Shadrach, Meshach, and Abednego. My hair was singed, my skin blistered and bleeding, and there was the smell of fire and smoke. But I was alive and stronger than ever before. It was time for healing and restoration, but retirement will have to wait, for there is still much work to do. I have to share Denise's and my story with all who are willing to lend me their ears, minds, hearts, and souls. For there is a greater cause, the cause of the Living God. And he wants to hear from you.

Under The Big Oak

I've had my share of heartache.
I've felt the sting of pain
From standing out in the desert
Praying for rain.
I've seen my lonely teardrops
Fall down my lonely face.
Oh, how I long to hear the
Thunder roll again.

FFH, "Open up the Sky"[3]

It was a dark time of my life when I first came to know Denise. I had been in a committed relationship for over ten years. My first wife decided one day that she'd had enough and was moving on or should I say, moving out. Our marriage had been rocky, to say the least, but I thought we'd always be together and work out our problems.

Apparently, she had already begun a new relationship and was ready for a new start. I was devastated, we had spent so much of our young lives together, built a small and successful business together, and had made it through some pretty difficult times. I couldn't go to sleep at night; the pain was more than I could stand, so I took to drinking my Amaretto De' Sarona each night to turn my pain into laughter and then finally fall asleep. The laughter came from talking to my trusty and loyal dog, Spike, as I would tell him how women were no good and we didn't need them anyway. As I would sit there in the dark and discuss the meaning of life with Spike, eventually laughter would overcome me, as I would realize the ridiculous and pitiful reality of my life and situation. At least I had not lost my sense of humor.

My restaurant Ruscito's kept me fairly busy, but most of my mornings and afternoons were free to do plenty of redfish and trout fishing in Cedar Key. I would go there, even in the dead of winter, and find peace and solitude along with an occasional keeper. I'd wake up before dawn and prepare the rods and the boat for my day. Then, on my way out of town, I'd stop by my bank to make the daily deposit from the restaurant.

My bank was unusual at the time in that it offered banking from seven to seven, so it was convenient for me to pull through there each morning, sometimes with my boat in tow. My wife always did the banking in the past, so I never noticed the cute girls there counting all that money. The youngest one was Terri, and the other one was a pretty young lady named Denise. I liked using the business lane because that way I could get up closer and get a good look at them. It was kind of like window-shopping, as I flirted with them and thought maybe one of these young ladies would be interested in me. My insecurities told me they would not want anything to do with an old man like me, I was just over thirty years old, and they both looked rather young. However, with my heart in the state that it was, I was not one to listen to my insecurities. I set my sights on Terri, the younger of the two, mostly because she was the more aggressive of the two and showed the most interest in me. Little did I know that both of them had found me a bit intriguing and were aware of my newfound single status.

One day I got up the courage to send Terri some flowers and ask her out on a date. I thought that surely the younger boys they were accustomed to would never be so bold and daring to send flowers to their place of employment. I'd hoped that Terri would be somewhat overwhelmed by the gesture and would be more willing to take a chance on a fool like me. What I didn't know was that Terri had a significant other and had actually been married and divorced by her young age of twenty-one. When she received the flowers, however, she was stunned and still considered accepting the date. She and Denise were actually roommates at the time so she naturally confided in her and asked her advice. Denise was a bit envious but kept her wits about her and explained that accepting this proposition was a terrible idea and that Terri should remember that she already had a man. Terri agreed, and so she called me on the phone, thanked me for the flowers and turned me down. I was disappointed to say the least, but that would not stop me from looking in the window for other candy that may still be available. I turned my attention to Denise over the next few weeks, found her interesting, and thought, *Why not give her a try, what do I have to lose?* If I made a complete fool of myself, there were other banks that I could take my business to. I learned that Denise was living on a large piece of property outside of Gainesville in a small town called Micanopy. She was renting the property from a friend she'd met in the Keys and shared the space with him and Terri. I pretended to be interested in the property, of course; everyone wants to buy acreage, but I had no real means to do so. Just the same, I thought this might offer a good opportunity to meet Denise in private and give us a chance to get to know each other and explore the possibilities. Denise had mentioned that the property was for sale and agreed to meet me out there to show it to me. I suggested we meet at the Clock Restaurant for breakfast, and then we could drive out to the property together. She agreed. My plan was working out perfectly.

When we finally made it to the property, we never even made it to the inside of the trailer. The outside was gorgeous, covered with natural, old Florida vegetation and huge beautiful live oak trees. To the left side of the driveway was an inviting bench parked beneath one of the most gorgeous, giant oaks I've ever seen. Its canopy provided shade and comfort for what would be one of the most intimate moments I'd ever had in my life. Denise and I opened up our lives to each other that afternoon. What seemed like ten minutes turned into two hours of sharing our trials and dreams with each other.

There was something about Denise, the way she talked to me that just reached deep into my soul and captured me. She was so honest, and when she looked into me with her soft brown eyes and spoke, my heart just simply melted. I thought, *There is no way I can leave this bench without first securing another date*. Trembling, I asked her if she would like to go out sometime, and her response surprised me and dashed my hopes.

She told me that she was seeing someone right now and really didn't think it would be right if she saw another man at this time. My mind was racing, and although I felt like this opportunity was slipping away, I knew that desperate times, called for desperate measures, something my ex-wife had taught me.

So I asked her, "What is his name?"

She replied "Bob."

Then I said, "This Bob fellow, do you love him?"

She thought about it for a moment and quickly said, "Well, no."

I explained to her that I really felt that there could be something "special" between us and did not think she should allow Bob to prevent her from harmlessly exploring it. I told her that I would like the opportunity to get to know her better and vice-versa and let the chips fall where they may. Denise and I began a new life together that day, and it will always be one of the most significant days of my life!

A New Beginning

Ordinary? No! I really don't think so,
Not a love this true.
Common destiny, we were meant to be,
me and you.
Like a perfect scene from a movie screen,
We're a dream come true.
Suited perfectly, for eternity,
me and you.
Kenny Chesney, "Me And You"[4]

On one of our earlier dates, for Denise's twenty-third birth-day, a friend of mine, Jimmy Swartz took the two of us skeet shooting. I had done some shooting in the past, but little ole Denise had never fired a gun of any kind whatsoever. Boy, did we have a blast! Denise did surprisingly well too, blowing away several clay pigeons that day. However, what I remember most about that day is finding out just how tough Denise really was. Let me explain. After the shooting, Denise and I loaded up into my truck to go and have some lunch. I noticed that her right shoulder and bicep had what was probably the ugliest bruise that I have ever seen. This thing was green, purple, black, and blue and stretched from the inside of her elbow to the top of her shoulder!

I asked, "What in the world happened to you?"

She proceeded to tell me that when she fired the first shot she forgot to hold the butt of the twelve-gage shotgun tightly against her shoulder, and the kick slammed into her shoulder like the impact of a jab from Mike Tyson.

"But you never mentioned it or complained about it, doesn't it hurt."

She grimaced and replied, "Yes, it hurts like you know what, but I just didn't want to spoil our fun."

This is one tough lady, I thought to myself.

On another date, I took Denise to Cedar Key for some trout fishing. I'd never caught many that had much size to them, but they were pretty plentiful on the flats out there and provided plenty of action on a good day. Denise was fishing off the backside of the poling platform when she started yelling, "I got one! I got one!"

She was yanking the pole all over the place and I calmly said, "Stop jerking the pole all around, honey; you're going to rip his lips off!" We were laughing as I grabbed the net and looked down in the water to see the biggest trout I'd ever seen! I told her that if I ever played a fish like that it would've been gone in an instant. We had many laughs out there that day. What a joy it was to spend time with Denise.

Over the years to come, Denise and I spent many fun-filled hours on those waters, even when our children were infants. We'd take them out there, pitch a tent on one of the oyster covered islands, and fish the day away. At least until we bought our pontoon boat then our boat became our tent and island all in one.

After having courted each other for about six months,

Denise and I decided to get married. We thought it would be romantic to run off to Gatlinburg to get married. We found an adorable little white chapel there, and tied the knot good and tight. We rented a condominium on a little creek there and spent a few days there after the wedding.

One really cool thing happened there though; Denise met her father's mom, Beulah, whom she had never known. She found out about her a few weeks before our trip and spoke to her on the phone. I don't know why it was such a big secret, but no one had ever told Denise she had a grandmother in Clyde North Carolina. When we went to see her, she was the sweetest thing, probably ninety years old and weighed just less than one hundred pounds.

She shared stories about Denise's father with her and explained to her why he never saw Denise after he left the home. It seems he had previously started another family and just couldn't handle being in two places at the same time. His wife was extremely jealous and possessive and finally wouldn't stand for any more excursions away from home. She gave Denise some pictures of her father and some jewelry and then came the big surprise. She went to her bedroom and returned with what appeared to be a beautiful wedding gown. She referred to it as a cocktail dress from her days as a socialite; it was gorgeous and all white. She told Denise it would be an honor if she would be married in it, and Denise was glowing like a candle. She tried it on, and it would fit like a glove! I was a little uneasy because I knew I had only brought my nicest pair of blue jeans and a sport coat to wear to our little wedding and knew I'd be way underdressed and out-classed. But I thought, *Hey, this won't be the last time Denise out-shines me.*

She looked beautiful on our wedding day in that incredibly wonderful dress. Denise was strong, tough and honest but she was also sensitive, passionate and beautiful, and I'll never forget her and all she brought into my life. A few months later Beulah would die in her sleep, and I knew we would always remember our visit with her that day as very special.

One year later, our daughter Raechel was born, the most perfect baby I had ever seen in my life. Denise had been in labor for fifteen hours. She had to be induced because Denise's placenta was not co-operating and they said the baby was in distress. Denise wanted to have natural childbirth, and what a nightmare that was. I'll never understand why some women think they need to experience the real pain of childbirth, but Denise was adamant about it and didn't want the epidural. Eight hours in it, things were getting very difficult, for both of us. Denise was having excruciating back pain and was having me rub her back until her skin was raw and my huge hands were worn out.

She kept yelling at me, *"Rub it like you mean it; rub it like you mean it!"* We had a lot of laughs about that later on but not right then. A couple of hours later she gave in and finally asked for some pain medicine. I don't know what they gave her, but it made her sick as a dog. Now, not only was she in terrible pain, but she was throwing up between contractions! I was thinking, *Somebody wake me up from this nightmare.*

About that time a friend of mine, Bob Gorman, came

by to see us and peeked his head into the room. He took one look and had this horrified look on his face and quickly exited stage right. Later he jokingly told me he thought Denise's head was going to spin around like the girl in the movie *The Exorcist.*[5] I told him, "So did I."

Once the drugs wore off we told the nurses we'd like no more of that, and Denise reluctantly ordered the epidural. I've never been more relieved about anything in my entire life. It seemed to take forever to get the procedure done in part because it was about three o'clock in the morning, and it took a specialist to do the procedure. Once it was done though, Denise fell right to sleep, and so did I. I was awakened abruptly the same morning around seven o'clock to be told that Denise was about to deliver and to get ready. I told the doctor, "Hold on man, I have to get the video camera ready!"

He looked at me like I was stupid or something and said, "Sorry, Rod, it doesn't work that way."

I turned the camera on and captured Raechel's birth on video. She was so perfect and beautiful. I was allowed to cut her umbilical cord, and the birth was documented at precisely 7:11 a.m., March 20, 1993. That would be the first time in my life that I had a glimpse of God and witnessed first hand one of His most amazing miracles that I would ever be a witness of.

Denise and I wanted to be the perfect parents and made some serious commitments during those early days of our family. Raising our children properly would take top priority. Denise's mother Dot was living with us then, and she was a big help with Raechel, even though she was still dealing with very serious mental health issues. We decided that Denise would keep her job at Gainesville State Bank. She worked an early shift—typically 6:30 a.m.–2:30 p.m. That worked out perfectly, as I worked my schedule so I would work evenings *only* from 3 p.m. to close and usually be home by 11 p.m. We vowed never to use a daycare and thought that if we were to raise a family then we were the ones who should do the raising. We would hand Raechel off to each other each day. Raising her was a total team effort. I had a lot of fun with Raechel in that time, playing on the swings in our house and at the park, feeding her, bouncing her, rocking her to sleep, even changing her dirty diapers was a joy. And she was an easy baby too; she was never colicky and very rarely did she ever get sick. She had big beautiful blue eyes that were as bright as the sun; I always knew Raechel was special.

The one thing we never got around to was going to church. Before Raechel was born I never had a reason to believe that God actually existed. In fact, while going through my separation with my first wife, I was extremely angry with life in general and thought that if there were a God, he was obviously out to get me and certainly was no friend of mine.

One night at the restaurant I walked to the back of the kitchen where our dishwasher, Kenny Brown, was hard at work. I told him that if a God existed then he was no good and I had no use for him. His eyes got real big, and he told me that I was crazy and I shouldn't talk like that. Kenny was a God fearing man. He said that God wouldn't like that and he would punish me if I didn't stop. I laughed and walked out the back door and looked up into the sky and challenged God. "Come on God, show me what you got! Why don't you throw a nice big bolt of lightning on me if you think you're so tough? You've punished me all of my life, why stop now, is that all you got!" Have you ever felt that way? Kenny didn't like it and asked me not to stand next to him as he did not wish to be a part of the collateral damage. Anyway, I look back on that day often now, and I think God was looking down on me with a sort of smirk on His face and while shaking His head gently back and forth He quietly said, "Nope." God had a plan for me and wasn't through with me yet. Thankfully, lightning wasn't part of the plan but he would strike just as quickly.

Denise enjoyed spontaneity. Sometimes we'd wake up on a Saturday morning, and I'd say, "Let's go to St. Augustine today and spend the night there."

She'd always say, "Sure, why not?" And off we'd go. On one such occasion, we made it there, and it was raining. For most people, the rain would ruin their day and perhaps spoil their entire weekend, not for Denise and me. I remember covering Raechel's carriage with a towel and the three of us going for a walk outside in the rain. It wasn't a downpour, and we were there, so we were going to make the most of it. We always believed in making lemonade from the lemons in our lives. Denise and I had fun chasing each other around and running with Raechel in her little buggy just playing tag in the rain.

We'd go have lunch, drive around in the truck, or sit in the hotel. It didn't matter as long as we were all there doing something together, as a family. To this day, St. Augustine remains my favorite city in the world.

Our son, Richard's, birth was much different from that of Raechel's. For one, we found out in advance that we were having a boy. That took some of the excitement out of the whole episode, I strongly recommend waiting for the doctor to yell, "It's a boy," or "It's a girl." In addition, Denise decided that natural childbirth was not in the cards for her and an early epidural would be a top priority. Also, since we had been through this all once before, it just didn't seem as exciting as it was the first time. I've discovered that's the way life is. Sometimes we just think we've seen and done everything, but you never know when one of life's curveballs will come at you at eighty miles per hour. We tend to take things for granted. Big mistake.

During Richard's delivery, the doctor calmly mentioned that the umbilical cord was wrapped around his neck and he wasn't breathing. I watched in horror as he calmly unwrapped the cord from around little Richard's neck. It must have been looped around three or four times. He quickly cut the cord himself and handed the newborn to the respiratory therapist. The doctor was so calm that I really did not get anxious right away. But then the respiratory therapist seemed to be in distress as she was trying to get Richard to respond. She was tapping his feet and his bottom, clearing his airway and looking for signs of life. I noticed Richard didn't look very well either. His body was colorless, and his face was blue. Finally, after what seemed like an eternity, he began to cough and gag and eventually scream and cry. It was music to our ears. He was quickly whisked away, and we didn't get to hold him until he was thoroughly checked out.

I didn't learn how to pray that day, but I should have.

However, I'm sure someone in that room was praying because obviously prayers were answered. Richard recovered and was a completely normal, healthy baby. He was born shortly before nine o'clock on a Monday night. I know this because the Giants were playing the Cowboys that night on Monday night football. I told our obstetrician Dr. Baily, "Let's get this going, Greg. I want to watch the game tonight and don't want to miss the kickoff."

Of course, I was only joking because I was a Dolphin fan. It was November 7, 1994; the kids would be just eighteen months apart, which was simply perfect!

Before Richard was born, we had another important decision to make. Should Denise continue to work? Could we afford to live on just one income? The restaurant was doing fine, but I didn't make a whole lot of money. For us, it wasn't a hard decision to make. Denise needed to be home with the kids to give them the care that only a mother is equipped to do. We were determined to give our children the life we never had, and if that meant doing without boats, nice cars, meals away from home, or whatever, so be it. Therefore, Denise would have to leave her job behind and I would have to get a second job to try to replace her income. I went out and bought an existing lawn care company. I figured I could do that during the morning and noon hours. It was really not a company, just some woman who had built up a dozen or so accounts mostly mowing their lawns and keeping them tidy; I could do that. And it was well worth it too, not only was it best for our children, but it was a dream come true for Denise.

Denise now had a stable husband, two beautiful children, a decent place to call home, her mom taken care of, and most important of all, a husband who loved her and was as committed to her as she was to him. Looking back now, I'm so happy with the decisions we made. Several times before she died Denise told me something that I'll never forget. "Thank you, Rod for making all of my dreams come true! I'll always love you for that." Looking back at this time brings much joy and satisfaction while I still struggle with my grief. However, there was still one thing missing from our lives. Do you know what it is?

A Wake-Up Call

> Empty again
> Sunken down so far
> So scared to fall
> I might not get up again
> So I lay at your feet
> All my brokenness
> I carry all of my burdens to you
> Jars of Clay, "Much Afraid"[6]

Life's funny. We all can get so busy from day to day that if you're not careful you can forget about the things that are important and begin to take life for granted. That's the way things became for Denise and I. I was working two jobs just trying to make ends meet, and Denise was home taking care of an infant and a toddler working hard to keep up with them and find some time for enjoyment at the same time. We were happy, but we were very busy and unsuspecting of what was coming for us around the corner. Kind of like rushing through traffic on the way to work, minding your own business but not completely paying attention just the same. Next thing you know, wham, somebody runs the red light and your day, with all you had planned, just goes right out the window.

A couple of months after Richard's birth, some lymph

nodes on the left side of Denise's neck become swollen. No big deal, probably from a cold or something. It was February, so colds were pretty common that time of year. Denise eventually made an appointment to see our family doctor, and they prescribed some antibiotics thinking it was some sort of infection. No big deal. A couple of weeks later the lymph nodes were not going away; were actually a little bit bigger. The doctor wanted to try a different antibiotic.

Two weeks later, the lymph nodes were still there and even a little bit sore to the touch. Our doctor, Dr. Lee-Pack thought Denise should go to see an ear, nose, and throat specialist. After another week or so we were together to see the ENT, Ann Jackson, and she advised us to have a biopsy just to rule out anything serious, like lymphoma or Hodgkin's disease. These are two common types of cancer related to the lymph glands. So, a week or so later we brought Denise down to the Ayers Medical Plaza for a simple procedure known as a lymph-node biopsy.

Interestingly, while we were in the waiting room, there was a code blue or something with Dr. Jackson's previous patient. We can see all of the nurses frantically running around and calling for an ambulance. The receptionist informs us that it was going to be a bit longer for us to wait due to the complications our doctor was having with one of her patients. Jokingly, I tell Denise that this was a good thing because, "What are the odds that our doctor would lose two patients on the same day?" It helped to break up the tension a little bit, and we were assured that this was a very simple, routine, out-patient procedure.

When we finally got to see Dr. Jackson, we could tell she

had had a tough morning. She said her previous patient's lungs were in very poor condition, and that had caused some complications. Trying to calm our fears, she said not to worry, that Denise would be a simple case, and she would be in and out. The procedure only took about forty minutes or so. Sure enough it went smooth as silk. Dr. Jackson said the tissue did not appear to be cancerous. Just to be sure, they would have to send it off to the lab, and the results would be back in a few days or so. We scheduled an appointment for the results, and that was that.

When the appointment finally came up, we decided that Denise would go and meet with the doctor alone and I would stay home and watch our children while she was away. I had a similar procedure done when I was in college, and all it turned out to be was a serious infection that the antibiotics were unable to touch for some unexplainable reason. So of course, I reasoned that this is exactly what was happening with Denise, and there was no reason to get ourselves all worked up over something that was nothing.

Denise was the picture of health; she almost never drank alcohol, never smoked cigarettes, never did any drugs, actually enjoyed eating fruits and low-fat foods and was in excellent physical condition. Her body-fat percent was probably below five percent. How could she have anything wrong with her? She was just twenty-six years old.

Denise's appointment was for two o'clock. As it was fast approaching five o'clock, I began to worry. Finally, the phone rang, and it was Denise calling me from the car phone, she was obviously distraught and crying uncontrollably.

"Rod, they said I have cancer and have six months to one year to live!"

"What?" I asked in disbelief.

"I have cancer, melanoma skin cancer! They said it was totally unexpected because we did not find it on the skin. It is worse than the worst case scenario that we had talked about!" Denise sobbed.

"Skin cancer, that's not life threatening," I said. "What in the world are you talking about? Where are you? Just come home. Hurry home and give me their phone number. I need to talk to that doctor. What's her name? Her name is Ann. Yeah, that's it, Ann Jackson!" I tried my best to comfort my wife over the phone. "Honey, don't worry. We'll figure this out. There must be some mistake! Just hurry home and I'll be here for you. I love you." I cried into the phone and then hung up.

Frantically, I called the doctor's office and got the answering service. It was just after five o'clock, and the office was closed. I told them it was an emergency and to have the doctor call me back a.s.a.p. When the doctor called, I could not believe what she was telling me. She said that she just had no idea that Denise would come up with Melanoma, the deadliest form of skin cancer. She said she wished there was something she could do or say that would help us, but she simply did not know of anything that would help. She did give one piece of advice: whatever we did, be as aggressive as possible.

When Denise got home, I didn't know what to say to her. I met her out on the front porch. Both of us just started crying and holding each other and didn't know what to do. With my arms wrapped around her I slid down to my knees, crying into her stomach. "God please, please help me!

I can't do this without you. Please God, take *me*, take *me*, take *me* … I'll do anything you want God, just please help me God!" For the first time in my life, I asked God to help me. I asked him and really and truly meant it.

They say God can read your heart, and mine was shattered but honestly seeking him and all he had to offer. How could it be that this would turn out to be the most important day of my life? The first day of a new life, a life depending on and asking for a relationship with God. A God I never knew or deserved to know.

Much Afraid

All said and done I stand alone,
Amongst the remains of life I should not own
It takes all I am to believe
In the mercy that covers me.
Did you really have to die for me?
Jars of Clay, "Worlds Apart"[7]

Denise and I needed a few days to sort things out and try
to figure out exactly what had just happened. A car had just
broadsided us, and we were lying in the ditch thinking, *Where
in the world did that come from?* There was a moment of utter
and complete silence, pieces of wreckage were scattered all
about us. There was blood on my forehead that didn't seem
to be coming from anywhere in particular, and my life was
flashing before my eyes.

One of the first things I did was to seek information. I
just had to know exactly what I was dealing with. The optimist in me thought that surely there had been some mistake.
After all, this was skin cancer we were talking about. How
could skin cancer be so deadly? Denise and I decided to take
a trip to the local public library and look up all we could
find out about melanoma. What a sobering experience that

turned out to be. All the information I could find pointed to certain disaster. The data showed that most people who have Stage II melanoma, melanoma that has traveled beyond the skin and into the lymph system, never live for five years or more. In fact, five years is considered long-term survival, and only five percent of the victims make it to see five years! If a patient could make it for five years, cancer free, then the odds for longer survival increases dramatically. The problem is in getting to the five-year mark without ever having more cancer. I spent the rest of the day sitting on the park bench outside the library with my wife and crying like a baby. We had come seeking information and found nothing but hopelessness and dead ends. *Great*, I thought, *this is not going to be easy.* In fact, survival was going to be nearly impossible.

Denise and I cried almost constantly together for the next three days. After that, Denise pulled herself together and said, "Okay, that's it. I'm not going to cry about this any more. We've had our pity party, so now it's time to get on with things."

I thought, *You're right. We can't just sit here and cry like babies. We have to do something about this.* But I also realized that there was so much at stake. This was not just about a single person battling a disease to save her life. This was about raising children and family. This was an all-out assault on the institution of marriage, family, and everything that is important in life. It occurred to me that people threw away their families every day. Denise's family did it when her dad left her and her mom high and dry when Denise was just three months old. My family had done it, breaking off their marriage after fifteen years with four children left to be raised by a single parent. This was such an important part of who Denise and I had become. More than anything else in the world, we wanted to have our very own family that we could raise with the love and wholeness that we never received as children. Though we had parents who loved us, our families were not intact and could not provide us with the type of family life that God had intended. We had been determined to provide just that for our children. We would not stand for having any kind of separation or situation where our family was not only together but loving and intact physically and emotionally. We never considered something like this, something we had absolutely no control of. Only God could help us now!

I'll Do Anything

I'll do anything
To make you see what I'm imagining
To know the pleasure your smile can bring
To keep the light from vanishing
Jackson Browne, "I'll Do Anything"[8]

Once the crying was over, it was time to get busy. The clock was ticking, and I knew it. All I had learned about cancer so far told me that the cells multiply exponentially, much different from the way a normal cell divides, one by one. I couldn't help but think that each and every day those cells were in there just multiplying and making whatever treatments we could find less and less likely to succeed.

The first thing I did was to get on the phone and to continue to search for information. Denise called the hotline for the American Cancer Society who promised to send us all the info they had accumulated on melanoma. I talked to my stepmother's ex-husband, King Smith. She had mentioned that he was a doctor, and I really didn't know where else to start. He said he knew very little about melanoma other than how devastating it was, but he did recall a pathologist that he worked with. Dr. Smith said he thought he was fairly knowledgeable on the subject, so he gave me his name and number.

When I spoke to the pathologist, he was the first one who gave me any encouragement whatsoever. He said that the disease was incredibly difficult to treat; however, there were some known cases where people had survived the disease and gone into long-term remissions. The problem was that nobody understood why this would happen for some and not others. At least I felt that there was some hope and that was all I needed to keep motivated. He shared some ideas and some names and phone numbers of some of the researchers who were at the forefront of the melanoma research.

About the same time, we received some information from the ACS along with a book titled, "There's Hope" written by Richard Bloch of H&R Block, the well-known tax consultants. He had been diagnosed with terminal lung cancer and given an extremely poor prognosis. However, he decided to fight and be aggressive and was actually able to beat his disease through some very aggressive therapies. What was nice about the book was not only the inspiration it provided, but the detailed information on how he went about fighting his disease. I took all of this advice to heart and began the journey.

One of my most favorite singers of all time is Jackson Browne. He is known as "the King of Pain" because he has suffered a great deal in his life and wrote lyrics that pulled the deepest substance from inside the heart. As I read the lyrics to "I'll Do Anything" it reopens deep, emotional wounds that sometimes bring tears to my eyes. This song in particular is amazing to me because I can relate to it so perfectly. It aptly describes his desperation to want to save someone he deeply loves. Perhaps his struggle is not about life or death, perhaps it is a simple break-up with a girlfriend or a wife, but it is intense and deep just the same. For me it is about saving the life of someone that is more important to you than your own life itself and that all that is worth living for is being held hostage.

> You hold a life there in your hands
> You probably don't know
> Somehow your dreams became my plans
> Somewhere long ago
> Think about the things we've done
> and where we've been
> Your touch made me a king
> I don't want to live without your love again
> I'll do anything[9]

In his interpretation, I'm sure he is talking about how this other person holds his life in her hands. That is not what it means to me. The song is telling me that I hold Denise's life in my hands, and that her ultimate survival will be my responsibility. That is a pretty tall order for someone who makes pizza for a living, but I will do anything! The last part of the verse is what really gets to me however. "Your touch made me a king." That is exactly how Denise impacted my life, and I could not imagine living without her, knowing that the kingdom would fall if she were not in it.

My responsibility went way beyond just finding the right medical care and working hard to rescue her and saving her life. What mattered was doing that and at the same time having a life that was worth fighting for. A life that was more fulfilling than any we had known before. Not only for finding happiness but making the world a better place to be.

Fighting Back—Maryland

She is strong enough to stand in your love.
I can hear her say
I am weak. I am poor,
I'm broken Lord but I'm yours.
Hold me now.
Jennifer Knapp, "Hold Me Now"[10]

I couldn't believe we had to wait two weeks for an appointment with our oncologist. I wanted to ask the doctors, Do you all understand just how fast the cancer reproduces? It made me wonder, *Are these guys really just that busy, or is it that they just don't care*? Either way, it didn't really matter because they had us over a barrel. I could not sit still waiting to meet the man who was going to save Denise's life, so I got busy with doing research. One thing I had going for me was the ability to use a computer. I learned from Block's book that getting the PDQ from the American Cancer Society was imperative. This PDQ or physicians desktop query would be a valuable source of information. I learned what our options were going to be and was able to start doing research on what looked to be working for other melanoma patients and what did not work. The options were basically this: surgery to remove the lymph nodes (this would be known as a complete neck dissection), radiation (apparently low-dose radiation had been proven ineffective, and they were experiencing some success with higher doses), interferon alphatherapy (a natural substance produced by the immune system but delivered subcutaneously by injection several days per week), experimental vaccine therapy (a relatively new approach that had created much excitement in the melanoma community), and nothing. That's correct, nothing. There was some evidence to suggest that even if you did many of the advanced therapies, it did not seem to make one iota of difference, and interestingly, if you did some specialized therapy and achieved results, you still could not be sure what exactly it was that made a difference, if any.

I began searching the Internet for solutions. I've had enough of the problems. Most of my time was spent looking at the various clinical trials through the many Web sites available to me. Typically, the National Cancer Institute had the broadest amount of information, and I found their Web site easy to manipulate. What I found most helpful really was the information given at the end of the trial information. This was where the doctors or principle investigators were listed along with their phone numbers. I thought, *What do I have to lose? Why not just call some of these guys and see if they will talk to me?* I looked for the doctors whose names appeared on more than one trial and seemed to be associated with some of the more prestigious and larger hospitals. Places like MD Anderson in Houston, Sloan Kettering in New York and the John Wayne Cancer Center in Santa Monica, California.[11]

As I began to make the calls, I was amazed at how interested some of them were in finding out more information about Denise. I later realized that not only did we need them, but they needed patients to advance their research. The only complication being, *Did the patient fit in with their criteria?* A patient could be excluded from a clinical trial for many various reasons. It could be their disease was either advanced too much or not far enough. It could be that they had removed the tumor, and a tumor was needed in order to see results. Or perhaps, the patient had taken another drug that interfered with their particular trial. It can really be quite complicated, and I could see where if we were not careful, we could very easily eliminate ourselves from a very good trial.

I learned that surgery was probably imminent and a very good option. With each option chosen, it seemed that the patient's chances for long term survival would improve, perhaps by as much as ten to twenty percent. I thought, *If we do surgery and gain twenty percent, then do radiation for another ten percent and interferon for fifteen percent, and a vaccine adds another twenty percent, then, hey, we just increased our odds by a whopping sixty-five percent!* Makes perfect sense right? Well, of course not, but I was in the restaurant business!

As I talked with the researchers, there was always one question I would ask them right before hanging up with them. "If this were your wife, what would you do?" I liked putting them on the spot, and I wanted them to think about what it would be like for them if they were in my shoes. I was a little surprised at how many of them answered this question.

And what I found was a common denominator … vaccine! Pretty much every one of them thought that current vaccine trials offered the most hope for a cure. Interferon Alpha A was another good option as research was revealing some effectiveness. Mostly, they found the interpheron only added about one year to the patient's life, on average. I thought, *Hey, an extra year is a lot when you look at the alternative.*

The problem was that many of the vaccine trials were closed and had all the patients they needed, or they were in the early stages and were very unproven. One day, I was talking with a Dr. Phillip Livingston from Sloan Kettering about his vaccine trial and the results he had seen. When I pressed him about his trial, he told me that his trial was no longer taking new patients, at least temporarily. I asked him my favorite question and added to it, "If you could not give your wife your vaccine, where would you send her?"

That was when he mentioned the John Wayne Cancer Institute in Santa Monica. He said that their trial had been ongoing for several years and they had seen some impressive results. *Good enough for me*, I thought. Once I hung up with him, I called out there, and they agreed to fax me a ten-page report explaining all about their trial, how to get in, and what results they had been seeing. I put it in with my notes and saved it for my meeting with our oncologist, so he could have a look and tell me his thoughts. I was hoping I wouldn't need to though; I was hoping he was going to have some good news for us and just begin some kind of helpful therapy that nobody else knew about. The optimist in me was working harder than the realist, but it kept me going.

My optimism faded very soon after we first met. Dr.

Vernon Miller, a sharp-looking man dressed in an Armani suit, came into the room and introduced himself to us. He sat down and told us he was sorry about our situation, but there were not any treatments that he was aware of that would do us very much good. He mentioned that he did his residency at the NIH in Maryland and knew of some very bright people there that could be helpful to us, but he wasn't sure if we were willing to take the time and effort to go there. He said he could arrange it, but we may have to stay there for a couple of weeks for testing and such. I quickly assured him that there was no place too far or inconvenient to us, and we were willing to do whatever it takes to provide Denise with the best opportunity for a cure as we could find.

At that, he said he would be right back and left the room to make some phone calls. I was disappointed but felt good in knowing that at least he was willing to put us in touch with someone who might know more than he did. Perhaps our situation was over his head and he recognized that, at least he was willing to admit it. Thirty minutes or so later he walked back into the room and told us he would make the appointment for us as soon as they could arrange all the details, but that they would be happy to see us. I felt good that at least a door had been opened for us, and that was encouraging, even if it was just a small door.

Before leaving, I talked to him about several protocols I had discovered on the Internet and specifically mentioned how promising the vaccine at the John Wayne Cancer Institute appeared to be. He said he was unfamiliar with their program and felt more comfortable sending us to some people he had worked and trained with. However, he said he would look it over and save it for future reference.

A few days later, we received a call and were given our schedule for the trip to Maryland. We were going to a center in Frederick, Maryland, called the Biological Response Modifiers Program (BRMP), and would meet with their director Dr. Kopreski. I couldn't believe we had to wait thirty days for our appointment. Again, I was perplexed at the lack of urgency being shown for our situation. *What is wrong with this picture?* I thought I was caught up in an episode of the *Twilight Zone* or something.

Again, it was out of my control, and all we could do is wait, patience has never been one of my strong points. We had to make arrangements on where to stay and how to get there and such, and I certainly had time to do that. I also had to prepare the restaurant for my absence and needed some time to hire the help I'd need while away.

I went to see my good friend, Dean Poole, to talk to him about my predicament. Dean was my CPA so he was used to hearing about my problems and the jams I sometimes find myself in. When I mentioned a trip to Maryland, Dean said, "Hey, wait a second, my best friend in the whole wide world lives in Annapolis, and I'd bet my bottom dollar that she would just love to help you with a place to stay. Why don't I give her a call right now?"

Dean called his friend, Judie Glixner, and within minutes, Denise and I had room, board, nurture and care all wrapped up together with Judie and her significant other Pete. I felt awkward accepting such kindness from total strangers.

Nana came up from Ft. Lauderdale to help Dot with the

babies while we were away. We would be gone for two weeks, and Denise and I had never been separated from the kids for more than a few hours, so that was pretty different. We missed them before we even hit the Georgia border.

Judie and Pete were a tremendous blessing, except that Judie was pushing her macrobiotic diet on us as a form of fighting the cancer. Denise and I both agreed that we would rather die then to have to eat like that again; it was disgusting. If we were living our last months together, we had already decided that we were going to enjoy ourselves, so we kindly asked for real food from then on. As it turned out, Judy had a daughter who had suffered from a long rare illness, and she had spent much time at the NIH. That was why she really dove into nutrition and such because she new the true powers of the human body and its ability to heal itself. We shared a lot about faith and God's love for us, and enjoyed watching some videos of Bernie Siegel on his series called Love, Medicine, and Miracles. What a great story.

We also took some side trips around with them when we were not with the doctors and saw some beautiful sights together; Annapolis was a gorgeous place to visit. Frederick was a city out in the country and was also a beautiful area. We took some other visits out there to see wildlife and such at some of the state parks in the area. On the weekend, we actually found time to drive to Stroudsburg, Pennsylvania to visit my Uncle Butch and Grandma Kemmerer whom I had rarely seen. What a neat opportunity that was.

That was how life was becoming for Denise and I. We were beginning to take advantage of all that life had to offer, regardless of our circumstances. We would make the most of each day we had together, making delicious lemonade from the sour lemons of our lives.

After completing test after test with Dr. Kopreski, we finally came to the end of our visit, and it was time to make some decisions. We met in his office on that final Friday morning, and he laid our options out before us. "You have a very aggressive form of cancer, and the one thing I think you should strongly consider is a complete neck dissection to remove all active lymph nodes in your neck, beyond that the choices are not as clear. Radiation, interpheron Alpha A therapy, or a clinical trial such as a vaccine protocol are other options you have. What do you think?"

"What do I think?" I replied, "I think that I make pizzas for a living, and I came here for you to tell us what we can do to save Denise's life. That's what I think!"

Dr. Kopreski had a very serious look on his face and answered, "I'm sorry, Rod, but that's not how this works. You are in a situation where we don't know what to do, and only you can decide. All I can do is provide you with the information and educate you, but in the end, it will be your decision."

"Okay," I said, "I think I understand, so you want me to be the one to play God. In that case, I'd like to have the surgery, do the radiation, begin the interpheron treatment and proceed with the vaccine clinical trial."

"That's not possible," he said. "Doing radiation and/or the interpheron would eliminate you from the vaccine trial; it is part of the protocol. Surgery is an option, but you would have to begin the vaccine thirty to sixty days following the surgery or you would also be eliminated from consideration there."

When the meeting was over, we had decided to proceed

with the surgery and then begin their vaccine trial. The BRMP was in the midst of developing a new vaccine, and Denise would be one of the first in the trial. The only catch was that her disease was not advanced enough to be completely within the parameters of the protocol. However, Dr. Kopreski assured us that he could attain an exception from the FDA, and Denise could be included due to the desperate nature of her situation. Being that she was so young and had two very young children, he thought that would all be taken into consideration and would not pose a problem.

It was decided that Ann Jackson should be the one to perform the neck dissection since she was already familiar with Denise and was known to be a good surgeon in Gainesville. I was not happy about that, and I explained that I was not very fond of Dr. Jackson. She had really distanced herself from us since her diagnosis, and I felt like she did not want to get to know people that she was afraid were going to die. Kopreski convinced me to keep my personal feelings out of the equation and go with who can get the job done right. I concurred and figured I'd express my feelings to Dr. Jackson when the opportunity presented itself; right now there were more important issues to deal with, life and death issues.

We thanked Dr. Kopreski for his time and efforts and told him we looked forward to seeing him again in a few weeks when the vaccine was ready and Denise had healed from her surgery. I noticed a picture of his wife and child on his desk and told him he had a beautiful family. I reminded him of how fortunate he was to have them and their health and to be sure he never lost sight of that. He thanked me, and we were on our way.

Fighting Back–
Gainesville

It's been forty days and forty nights
Down the road of many trials
And I pray it's only for a season
'Cause in the wilderness and in the flood
You're the one I'm thinking of
And I know You've brought me for a reason
Third Day, "Forty Days"[12]

Once we were back in Gainesville, we did not have to wait long for Denise's surgery. Dr. Jackson had scheduled it while we were in Maryland, and even though I did not care for her bedside manner, she was one of the few doctors to this point that showed any sense of urgency. I was thankful for that. Before our pre-op appointment, I took the time to write her a three-page letter telling her how I felt about her emotional disappearing act. I had copied down the "doctors' creed" I found on a waiting room wall at the BRMP and put it in the letter. I told her that her distancing herself from us had stolen our hope and increased our anxiety over the situation, and this was not good for her patient. I added that if she were unable to deal with life and death issues that perhaps she would be better off as a dentist or podiatrist. Denise and I both noticed her distance from the situation and felt as if we had been stricken with some sort of plague or something, not a nice way to feel especially considering our situation. We were depending on these doctors to save us from drowning, and they were afraid to get too close as if we were going to grab onto them and take them down with us.

I gave her the letter shortly after she walked into the room but felt I needed to explain things to her in person. I wanted to hear what she had to say and did not want to simply blind-side her with an aerial attack. After all, she was going to be performing surgery on Denise, and I wanted to hear her side of things before that happened.

When she came into the room, I confronted her almost immediately. "Good morning, Dr. Jackson. How are you?" I began.

"Just fine," she replied, as she turned her attention toward Denise.

"Listen, Ann, there is something that has been on my mind since our last visit, and I've written my thoughts down in this letter I have here for you; I hope you will have time to read it later," I said, trying to calm myself. "It concerns the way Denise and I feel that you have distanced yourself from us since you diagnosed Denise with Melanoma. We feel like you are afraid to get close to us because of our situation, and that is causing us a lot of anxiety and stress, which as you know is not good for Denise."

She paused for a moment and turned her attention to a couple of pictures of a young lady she had on the table and mounted on the wall. "I'm sorry, this is very difficult for me,,"she explained. "The young lady you see here in these pictures was a patient of mine with whom I became very close. She came down with lymphoma, and I did all I could to save her, but instead, I became attached to her, and when she died, it was very rough on me. This all happened recently, and when I received the news on Denise, it was just all too fresh for me to allow that to happen again."

I considered her feelings for a moment, but then my love for Denise took over. "I'm sorry you had to go through that, but it is important to me that you know how you made us feel. Your job requires you to handle life and death situations and care for your patients regardless of your personal feelings. Denise and I felt abandoned by you, and that removed most of the hope we were searching for. Right now, hope is all we have, so we need all we can find. Please consider these things before you have to deal with another patient that finds themselves in a similar situation." We never brought the subject up again, and we did not bond after that day either. However, I do feel we gained a sort of mutual respect for each other, which was a good thing. We talked about the procedure that would take place the next day, received our instructions, and were sent on our way.

I was amazed at the number of people who showed up for surgery the next day. We had only been members of our new church, Trinity, for a short while, yet they sent several people over prior to the surgery to be with us and pray for Denise and I. Marvin McMillan was someone who spent a lot of time visiting sick members and was especially comforting to both of us. He had a certain kind of quiet calm about him, but I could also feel a sense of peace and strength about him. Dan

Johnson, the church pastor was also there, and I could just tell that he and Denise were forming a special bond together. He was also very calm and carried an aura of confidence that was quite comforting. It was as if he knew something we didn't, and everything was going to be just fine.

Sandy Miller was another prayer warrior who we connected with. She was a survivor of breast cancer and helped lead a cancer support group Denise had become involved with. She was also very calming and confident. I could tell she had some special connections with our creator, and it was good to know that she was on our side. Jean Evans was in charge of the children's ministries at Trinity, and we had come to know her because of our "precious little ones," as she so affectionately referred to them. Again, she was calm and had peace and quiet running through her. Our close friends, Tammy and Kevin Grosskopf, were also there and offered their love and support to us. It was really a neat thing to see unfold. We had begun to assemble our team of support. Doctors, pastors, friends, and family were all parts of the team who had their role to play, just like a quarterback, halfback, linebackers, and such all working together to win the big game. Just before they took Denise into surgery, we all gathered around her and formed a circle with our hands joined together. Everyone in the circle prayed for Denise out loud and without fear; It was awesome. They prayed for the surgeons and assistants. They prayed for God to be with Denise and keep her strong and to watch over and protect her. They prayed for a quick recovery and fast healing free from pain and infection. It was specific, sincere, and bold, and God was listening.

When I walked into the recovery room immediately following the surgery, I stood at the foot of the bed, as tears rolled down my face. Denise had been cut from the bottom of her ear to the top of her chest. The staples were large and nasty; I couldn't believe it. She had two tubes coming out of the wound with bulbs on the ends filling with fluids from the incision. She was still connected to the IV and other equipment, and I was not prepared for what I saw.

I stood there thinking, *Why can't I be laying there instead of her?* I wanted to take her pain and suffering from her any way that I could, but it was not possible. When she opened her eyes, she began to smile until she saw my tears. I think it frightened her to see me so upset because she thought it meant there was something wrong she didn't know about.

"Hey, honey, what's wrong, why are you crying?" she whispered.

"I just can't stand seeing you like this," I said. "I love you so much!"

"I love you, too, Rod; don't worry, I'm fine," she said quietly as the smile returned to her face. And fine she was; the surgery had gone perfectly and without any complications. Denise's recovery would be swift and nothing short of miraculous. She told the nurses she wanted to go home right away, but they forced her to stay overnight. When they came in to check on her the next morning, she had already dressed herself and told them to tell the doctor to hurry up because she was going home that morning. It was amazing, and so was my wife. Later that day, we were riding our bikes in our neighborhood, and Denise did not even need the pain medications they had sent home with her. She felt peace, strength, and comfort like never before.

Once the reports came back from pathology, we received some pretty bad news. The melanoma was very aggressive and had spread throughout the lymph nodes on the left side of her neck. Fifty-four lymph nodes had been removed and tested of which thirty-five tested positive. The doctors were clear that this showed an extremely aggressive Stage II melanoma that was quite active. I was not surprised. I felt the doctors had done everything they could to give the cancer plenty of time to grow.

The number of positive nodes greatly diminished any hopes we had for long-term survival and suggested greatly that the cancer had probably already spread microscopically to other regions of Denise's body. But at least we had finally done something and began the process of treatment that she so desperately needed. Maybe it wasn't too late, maybe there was hope, and maybe God was going to help us after all.

Fighting Back– California

The storm is wild enough for sailing,
The bridge is weak enough to cross,
this body frail enough for fighting.
I'm home enough to know I'm lost.
It's just enough to be strong.
In the broken places.
In the broken places.
It's just enough to be strong should the world rely
on faith tonight.
Jars of Clay, "Faith Enough"[13]

The plan from that point forward was to wait for Denise to heal completely. Then Denise would undergo some stress tests to see if she was strong enough to take the vaccine trial. The thought was that the vaccine would be ready to go in four or five weeks, and we would travel back to Maryland once the doctors there were prepared to begin the trial. Denise healed rapidly and without complications or infection. Two weeks later, we went over to North Florida

Regional Medical Center for the stress tests required by the clinical trial. Denise and I had a couple of very suspicious yet interesting conversations while there.

Denise met a young nurse who was helping her with the stress tests. She was a spiritual woman from the High Springs area and was a very committed Christian who attended the Baptist Church there. She was shocked that Denise was given such a terrible prognosis, as Denise showed no evidence of being sick, let alone having a terminal illness. As Denise worked on the treadmill, the young lady made a couple of interesting comments. "Denise, I don't even know you, but I have to tell you that I am getting a feeling that tells me you are going to be okay, that this is not going to be the tragedy that it appears to be. In addition, I need to tell you that there is a reason why you have the cancer and not your husband. You can handle this; your husband could not. You have such a positive attitude and are physically and mentally stronger than your husband is, so just know that you can make it through whatever comes your way. Don't ever give up."

Denise told me of their conversation once she was finished with the tests. She said it was pretty odd because the woman said she felt like God had asked her to tell Denise these things.

While sitting in the waiting room, I had an interesting encounter of my own. A middle-aged black gentleman approached me as he was passing by. "Hi, how are you?" he asked with a broad smile.

"Just fine. How 'bout yourself?" I casually responded.

"Well, I'm doing just great, thanks for asking young man," he fired back. "What brings you here today, if you don't mind my asking?"

"Well, my wife has been diagnosed with melanoma, a form of deadly skin cancer, and she is here taking some tests to see if she qualifies for a vaccine trial. We are actively seeking any kind of treatment that could be of help to her."

"Wow, I am so sorry to hear that. How old is she, and what is her name?" he asked as the smile left his face. "Her name is Denise, and she is just twenty six-years old. Kind of hard to believe, isn't it? We have two very young children, six-month-old Richard and two-year-old Raechel. As you can imagine, we are in a pretty desperate situation right now, and we are just searching for answers," I said. The man paused for a moment as he considered the gravity of the situation. I felt bad for a moment. I thought, *I probably shouldn't have laid all that on a stranger, but it felt kind of good to talk about it with someone I don't know.* I thought it was sort of interesting to see his reaction and to listen to what he had to say.

He folded his arms and said, "You know I have an idea of something that could be a big help to your wife Denise. Would you like to know what it is?" he asked.

"Absolutely," I responded as hope began to fill the air, "I'll do anything."

He said, "Well, okay then, here it is. When you go to bed at night and your wife falls asleep, lay your hands across her back and pray!"

That's it? I thought to myself. *This is the best he could come up with?* I was hoping for so much more. I thought maybe this guy was aware of some great treatment that I had not found in all of my Internet searching. Sometimes it really sucks to know everything. "Oh, well, hey, thank you for that advice. I will definitely try that starting tonight," I said as I forced a smile to my face.

The man had been very nice and was being sincere, so I did not want him to see my disappointment. "Well, good luck to you and your family. Take care and God bless you," he said as he went on his way.

"Same to you," I replied. *What a kook*, I thought to myself. *And to think he was going to know something that was going to save Denise's life. What a joke that was and what a fool I was for thinking it.*

A few weeks later, I was getting anxious as we were waiting for the doctors up north to call us and tell us when we could start the treatment. I called once or twice, and they said that the vaccine was just about ready and they were waiting for the FDA to give their final approval. Another few weeks went by and I was beside myself. I kept thinking about how Denise had such an aggressive form of the cancer, and we just continued to allow it to grow.

Finally, one day the phone rang and it was Dr. Kopreski. "Rod, I'm afraid I have good news and bad news," he said.

"Give it to me," I said sternly as I was in no mood to play games.

"Well, the vaccine is prepared and ready to go. That's the good news. The bad news is that the FDA is not going to grant the exception needed for Denise to participate in the trial. I'm very sorry," he said quietly.

"You have to be kidding me?! We've wasted all of this time for nothing! That is total garbage!" I yelled into the phone. "How in the world could you make us wait all this time and then tell me we can't participate in the trial. This can't be happening!"

"Rod, you have every right in the world to be upset. Please believe me when I tell you we did all we could to have Denise included in the study. I was so sure that they would grant us the exception we asked for, but they just felt like Denise's cancer is not advanced far enough along and did not want to put her at risk. If she advances to Stage III at some future time, we will definitely be able to include her. The door is not completely closed."

I thanked him for his efforts and hung up the phone. I was in a state of total shock and disbelief. My mind was reeling. *Now what are we going to do?*

I called Dr. Miller's office immediately to tell him the news. We were going to have to re-think everything now and come up with a plan B. Vernon was disappointed and said that we had wasted way too much time and really needed to do something right away. He said that we should just forget about the vaccine trials altogether and go straight to using the Interpheron Alpha A, a protocol which was the real standard of care for melanoma anyway. The problem was my research had revealed that the Interpheron protocol really had not been that successful. And not only that, it was very toxic and would make Denise quite ill while she was taking it. The protocol called for her to take three injections per week, and if it did what we hoped it would do, her life expectancy would be increased by just one year. A year was better than nothing, but the promise held by a vaccine trial could bring about a cure. That was a huge long shot, but at least it was a chance for something worth fighting for.

I asked Vernon what had happened to the fax I'd given him from the John Wayne Cancer Institute. He said he still had it but had not done anything with it. I asked him if he would please call them and find out if it was a good option for us. I asked him if he would also look for all other options available to us and we could discuss it as soon as he was able to schedule us for an appointment. He said he would do all of that and be prepared to go over everything with us just as soon as we could meet. He said he would have his secretary call me with the next available appointment. I agreed and hung up the phone.

I felt totally uneasy with Miller and just did not trust that he was working hard enough to help find the right treatment. He was in over his head, and I knew it. I had some time before our next appointment, so I figured I'd get back to searching the Internet.

One day, I discovered something that looked interesting to me. I learned of a hospital in Orlando that was connected to MD Anderson Cancer Center in Houston, Texas. I noticed some clinical trials held down there, and thought, *Why not give them a call? They're only two hours away;* it's worth a shot.

What happened next was incredible.

I called and asked to talk to the protocol nurse who was responsible for talking with patients connected to one of the trials they were conducting on melanoma patients. Susan asked me some general information, and I then explained to her my predicament and Denise's medical situation. Finally, I asked her if she had ever heard of the John Wayne Cancer Institute.

Much to my amazement she said, "Have I ever. I used to work there!"

"You're kidding me!" I shouted back to her. "Is it a good place for Melanoma patients like my wife to go to?"

"Absolutely," she responded. "We refer melanoma patients there quite regularly." I was in a state of total shock, and my spirits were lifted tremendously. She said we would need a referral, and I told her that would not be a problem. I gave her all of my information and told her we would be coming to see her very soon, and I hung up the phone. I wrote down all the information and stuck it in my wallet so I'd be sure to have it available when we met with Dr. Miller.

Our appointment with Dr. Miller did not go well at all, as I had suspected it would. The man was unable to get in touch with the John Wayne Cancer Institute. He claimed that he had attempted to call them but was unable to get through. He said there must be a problem with the phone number I gave him or something to that effect. It was ridiculous. He left the room and said he'd be right back; he was going to call them for us again and see if he could schedule an appointment for us.

He came back into the room and said, "Hey, they already know you down there." I told him that I had actually spoken with a protocol nurse who worked with Dr. Marsh out of MD Anderson in Orlando, and we would like to consult with them. I let him know that they referred many melanoma patients there on a regular basis and had good things to say about the vaccine trial. We left his office, happy to be going elsewhere and never saw Dr. Miller again.

The meeting with Dr. Marsh went terrific. "We've reviewed Denise's situation, and she is a perfect candidate for their vaccine trial. I've seen some surprising results for some of the patients we have referred there." He said optimistically. He then continued, "I believe the vaccine trial is absolutely the way to go and had you begun the Interpheron treatment at this stage you would have been disqualified for consideration of the vaccine. That would have been very unfortunate." He turned to me and asked, "Is traveling to California once per month going to pose a problem for either of you, Rod?"

"I have a Texaco credit card and a minivan, Dr. Marsh, and I'm not afraid to use them!" I replied with a chuckle. "We'll move there if necessary," I continued. "We are willing to do whatever we have to to provide Denise with the best treatment known to mankind, anything short of that would be unacceptable."

He called the JWCI and got the protocol nurse on the speakerphone. She asked us when we could be there, and I told her we did not wish to waste any more valuable time and we would be there for the next available appointment. This was on a Friday, and she said, "How's Wednesday sound for you?"

"Wednesday is perfect," I responded confidently. "All right then. Be there at 2:00 p.m."

"We'll be there with bells on," I said.

When I got home and started checking on flights, I was in for a real shocker. Flights without two weeks notice are not cheap; in fact, they wanted close to a thousand dollars each for us to fly to Los Angeles. Fortunately, I had some friends who worked for Delta Airlines, and they were able to pull a few strings for us. We were able to make the trip for about $450 each, still a lot of money for me, but at least it wouldn't max out my credit card. I called Judy and Pete to let them know where we were headed, and it just so happened that Judy had a very good friend who lived in Mission Viejo, California who she thought would be interested in helping us. Her name was Cookie, and she had lost a husband recently to cancer and that motivated her to help others touched by the same nasty illness, things continued to be looking up. My mom agreed to come up from Ft. Lauderdale to help Dot look after baby Richard and we decided to take Raechel with us since we would be there for two weeks.

Denise and I always made the most of our trips, whether they were for treatment or pleasure. California would be no exception. Mission Viejo was beautiful, and Cookie was the sweetest lady I've ever met. We saw the sights there and then went to our appointment with the doctors at the JWCI in Santa Monica. Denise had to undergo a skin test that would take five days to receive the results. She was injected with TB, and then they had to wait the five days to see how her body responded. Without the correct response, Denise would be excluded from the trial. There was some anxiety about that. But that was just part of the deal, and we accepted it.

For five days, we had nothing to do, so we rented a car, loaded our things and Raechel, and drove down to the San Diego zoo for a day. Then, we decided to see as much of the California coastline as possible in four days, and we drove it from San Diego to Carmel. What a wonderful time we had! By far the most gorgeous piece of real estate I've ever seen.

When we came back to Santa Monica we came through some of the wine country and enjoyed seeing the hills and countryside where much of the wines of California are produced. I even made a little side trip to see the Bundy estate where O.J. Simpson was accused of murdering his wife, Nicole Simpson, and her friend, Ron Goldman. Denise thought I was being morbid, and she did not join me on a walk up to the entrance, but I had spent countless hours watching the trial from my restaurant and was curious. Their home was only five minutes from the JWCI, so I thought, *Why not?*

After the five days, Denise passed the skin test and received the first round of injections of vaccine. She would get two shots under each armpit and on each side of her groin, eight injections all together. The TB added to the vaccine would cause the areas to blister badly, but that was the only adverse side effect and was quite tolerable. All that was left was for Denise to make the trip on her own once per month. Denise would become a very experienced traveler. The only real problem would be the expenses involved. The JWCI would pay for all the medical treatments associated with the vaccine, as experimental treatments are not covered by insurance. However, we would have to cover flights, hotels, meals, taxis, gas, etc, and this would become a problem. I was very concerned about whether or not I could afford all of it, as we pretty much spent all we made already.

I was deeply concerned over finances and even more so about my own state of mental health. I was dealing with the pressures of keeping Denise alive, and at the same time, I had the usual pressure of providing everything for my family: food, clothing, shelter, and even entertainment. I was also concerned that if Denise died suddenly, as the experts all agreed would most likely happen, that I wasn't going to be able to raise two children as a single dad and manage a restaurant at the same time.

I knew that when problems would come up for Denise I was going to need time off for surgeries and sick times, so I thought it might be best if I had a regular job where I could ask for time off when needed. Spending time away from Ruscito's had already taken a toll on the business, as I was relied on heavily there. Taking long vacations was not part of the business plan for running your own restaurant. The staff did the best they could, but I had to be there much more for it to be profitable. Besides that, I was concerned that if Denise died, I might just crack under all the pressure and just not come to work at all anymore. If that happened, I'd probably lose the business and forfeit its value altogether, so I decided to sell.

It took several months to accomplish, but I sold the restaurant for $135,000. I thought that was a lot until I paid the broker and all the bills and had nothing left. I accepted a down payment of $35,000 and roughly $2000 per month in payments which would come in handy as a supplement to my lower wages from the job I took selling food for Sysco Food Service, which was about half of what I was pulling in from the restaurant. I also had about eight thousand dollars in equity in my house, so I sold it also and moved the family into an apartment. It was a new development and very nice but a little expensive. My thinking was that Denise would probably die there, and I wanted her to be able to enjoy her time with the kids. The complex had a nice pool and clubhouse and was very convenient to shopping and our church, so it was perfect and worth the extra money. My boat would also have to go, so I sold it to a friend and made just enough to pay off the note it carried.

The last thing I owned that had any cash value at all was my truck. That was the most difficult thing I had to do. I had worked so hard to buy the Ford F-150 SuperCab. It was loaded with captain's chairs, electric everything, and even a moon roof. The dealer I bought it from said, "Nobody puts a moon roof in a truck!"

I said, "Oh, yes, they do, just watch me." It was my pride and joy and kind of a symbol of how hard I had worked in life to achieve some of the finer things. But in the end, life was not worth living without my wife and an intact family, so it also had to go. I traded it in on a used Ford Escort that I could barely fit into. *How awful that was.* However, my job called for a lot of driving, and I wanted good fuel economy to keep expenses low and good fuel economy was about all this little car was good for. At six foot two and 260 pounds, I looked pretty ridiculous and was very uncomfortable in the little car.

There was one last thing I owned that I could use to help fuel our battle with cancer, life insurance. I learned through *Coping* magazine that people with terminal illness could actually sell their policies at a discounted amount depending on the seriousness of their condition and their odds for survival. It was something that had been brought on by the AIDS epidemic that was sweeping the country. I owned two policies, one for fifty thousand and another for one hundred thousand.

I talked to a company about the fifty thousand dollar policy and they offered me seventeen thousand for the policy. They would continue the payments, and when Denise died, they would have a windfall for the other thirty-three thousand, not a bad deal for them if she died as expected. It was a tough choice, but I sold the policy and added the money to our war chest. I figured I still had the other policy to keep as a death benefit for the kid's sake when the time came. I wanted to be able to enjoy life as much as possible, and I knew that if Denise could have some fun and live stress free that this was really good for her physically and mentally and could even serve as a way of keeping her alive. It was well worth it!

Shortly after moving into the apartment, an interesting thing happened. One day a young couple pulled up with a moving van and was bringing their things into the apartment right next door to us. Denise mentioned that the husband looked like he had a cast on one arm and probably could use some help moving in. Denise was always thinking about some-one else. I admired that about her, but it usually meant more work for me, *oh well*. I went out and offered my services, and the young man was glad for the help. As it turned out the couple was Shane and Stephanie Mathews a well-known couple in Gainesville. Shane had an impressive career as the Gator quarterback for four years at the University of Florida and was beginning his new career in the NFL. Soon, we got to know both Shane and Stephanie, and Shane made us a very generous offer. He said that he regularly put on Golf benefits for different causes, and he wanted to dedicate the next tournament to Denise to help with the expenses of flying to California each month! The tournament raised about six thousand dollars and was used to pay off some medical expenses and some flights. But the tournament also caused the local paper to do a story on our situation and opened the doors for other people to help out also. An account was set up that people could donate their frequent flier miles into, and we could use those to purchase any future tickets. We never paid for another flight over the entire five years Denise was flying to California!

Much to our delight and amazement, Denise was cruising along without any complications or new cancer being found. She was very happy and enjoying her time as a mother and homemaker. I was really struggling though as I hated my job and had a difficult time adjusting to working for others. I had been self employed for over ten years and longed to be my own boss. The sacrifices I had made were taking their toll on me emotionally, and I knew it. I was becoming more and more depressed, and I realized I had to do something about it. I had no desire to work or play, even an opportunity to play golf or go fishing didn't interest me.

I decided I needed some help, and Denise encouraged me to see a psychiatrist. I made two visits, and before I knew it, he had prescribed Zoloft. I was kind of hoping he would be more interested in talking to me, but he did not seem interested in that. What he wanted to do was treat the symptoms and not worry so much about what was causing them.

The drugs made me feel strange, so I flushed them down the toilet and never saw him again.

Fortunately, Denise and I had attended a Christian retreat called Emmaus, and the people who went to this retreat were offered small groups that they could attend and talk about life's struggles so I joined one such group that our pastor from Trinity belonged to. What a difference this group would make in my life! We would pray and then talk about our closest and furthest moments to and from God. It was so cleansing for me and brought me closer and closer to God. Within six to eight weeks, my state of mind was totally different, and I felt like myself again.

The twelfth visit to California was a huge event in this clinical trial. If you could go twelve months without any recurrence, you could start taking the vaccine every three months instead. When Denise's anniversary approached, she made plans to lay over in Atlanta on the way home to relax and celebrate with my younger sister. Unfortunately, things did not go as planned. The doctors found some new cancer in her lymph nodes of her neck where she had her previous surgery, and they were going to have to be removed. Although the thought was that this could actually be "old" cancer left behind from the first surgery, it was still considered a recurrence and the vaccine would have to continue monthly for another year; Denise was devastated and so was I. She called me on the phone, and we agreed that she should forget about staying in Atlanta and come straight home. What transpired on her way home would change our lives forever.

Denise boarded her plane in Los Angeles and was very upset about all that had transpired. As she took her seat, she noticed a man who sat a few rows behind her carrying a Bible. Denise felt alone, afraid, and asking for God to comfort her. She thought perhaps the man was a pastor or at the very least was very spiritual, so she passed him a note and asked if he would come and pray with her. He never did. Denise was feeling abandoned, all over again, and the old wounds of abandonment were being reopened and making her angry. While waiting in the Atlanta airport, she had a brisk conversation with God and told him that if he did not give her a sign that he was still with her that she was going to give up on him altogether and throw away the faith that had begun to grow inside of her. Just at that moment, she heard a familiar voice standing behind her and she turned to see who it was. It was none other than our pastor of Trinity, Dan Johnson! Denise rose to greet him. He recognized her and was just as surprised as she was. Neither of them knew what God was up to, but they were about to find out. Dan noticed that Denise had been crying and asked her what was wrong. Denise explained all that had happened and how she had felt that God had abandoned her. Dan offered prayer and anointing with special oil he carried and asked if she would like to go somewhere more private. Denise said, "No way! Let's do it right here, right now." She knew that God had not abandoned her. In fact, he was delivering to her the sign that she so desperately needed!

Denise called me on the phone and told me all that had happened, and I was stunned. All I could say was, "Denise, if that is not divine intervention then I don't know what is!"

It was an occurrence that we would turn to often over the

years when doubts would enter our minds and hearts, and we would use it as a reminder of just how much God loves us and cares for us. We would also share it with others as we had hoped it would have a similar effect on their lives and help to increase their faith also. God is so good! Isn't he?

The newly discovered cancer in Denise's neck meant another surgery, the same as before. When Denise went to see Dr. Jackson, Denise said she looked as if she were seeing a ghost. Denise had lived over a year now and looked fantastic. This was not what Ann had expected, nor anyone else for that matter. I joked with Dr. Jackson that she should let me perform the surgery since all I had to do was cut on the dotted line; she wasn't amused. She may have still had a taste of my letter in her mouth, although she never mentioned the letter to me. The second surgery was a piece of cake. Denise came through the same as before, and we just knew this time that God had his hand on her.

We had even more prayer warriors than before, and people were coming out of the woodwork to help us with the kids, prepare meals, and just do anything they could to help. When Denise had the first surgery many people helped out and cooked meals for us while she was recovering. Denise got the idea from that experience to begin a ministry called "Feed the Flock." This was a more organized and coordinated effort to provide meals for people of the church who were struggling in some way. This way, everyone would receive this type of love and care, not just the ones who were thought of. It was a way that Denise could give back what she had received and was extremely successful. The ministry still exists today.

When Denise accomplished this, we were still very young in our faith and our church etiquette was not quite up to par. Denise was going to stand up in front of the congregation and tell them about the "Feed the Flock" ministry and ask for volunteers to help get things started. She dressed herself like a shepherd and carried a little stuffed lamb and a staff. After she gave her spiel, she looked at her watch and said, "Well my sheep are double parked and I'd better get the flock out of here!" You could have heard a pin drop, although there were a few chuckles amongst the silence. I think most everyone found it humorous but were simply too afraid to laugh. Our pastor Dan Johnson was stunned and could just see the e-mails and letters pouring in. One thing is for sure, it got their attention and woke a few of the pew-nappers, and I think Jesus was laughing too because I know he has a good sense of humor.

After her surgery, I spoke with Dr. Emmerson on the phone about being more aggressive in light of the possibility that this could be new cancer growth. My research told me that radiation to the neck region and even taking the Interpheron Alpha-A protocol while remaining on the vaccine would not be unreasonable. Much to my surprise, he agreed with me and approved of this course of action. We started the Interpheron almost immediately, and Denise was given injections subcutaneously three times per week. At first, she became very ill, flu-like symptoms were the norm, and dropped quite a bit of weight. After several weeks, she began to build up a resistance to the toxic substance and tolerated it fairly well. Many people who begin the protocol never finish the one-year trial but not Denise; she was determined to take the entire course and did just that. The radiation treatment was also quite difficult. We spoke with one radiologist who wanted Denise to begin a five-week regimen of low-dose radiation. I was a bit uncomfortable with this because I had read over and over that low-dose radiation was totally ineffective against melanoma. *Why would they prescribe it?* I met with a specialist from Shands, Dr. Bill Mendenhall to seek a second opinion. Coincidentally, Bill was also a member of Trinity UMC, and we would later become very good friends. He was a very soft spoken, kind man who could be recognized by his large collection of bow ties. Most people didn't wear these, but it was kind of an identity thing for Bill.

Bill agreed that low dose radiation was not really a good option in light of all we knew. He mentioned that he had heard of a new procedure being tried at MD Anderson in Houston called Fractionated Radiation. In this setting, the radiation was given in higher doses and less frequency. I think the total course was just five treatments every other day for ten days. Denise despised this treatment as much as anything she had been through. First of all, it burned the inside of her throat, and she was unable to eat or swallow much of anything, she was in quite a bit of pain for several weeks. Secondly, she had to place a large lead object down her throat while they delivered the radiation as a means to protect her throat as much as possible. She was not a happy camper, and she wanted everyone to know it. But this was good evidence of Denise's fighting spirit! She was willing to do "whatever it takes" to beat this cancer for as long as possible. She loved her children and me and was determined to keep our family together. She did not only want to stay alive but to live life to the fullest! And that is exactly what she did!

Denise continued the vaccine treatment for a total of five years. Her cancer eventually metastasized to her brain and this created a political problem for the FDA and the principle investigators of the trial with the John Wayne Cancer Institute. All told, Denise had made over sixty visits across the county to the JWCI, and she never missed a trip. Even through her radiation and Interpheron treatments, sick or not sick, she made those flights each and every time, and God provided.

Denise would make the ninety-minute drive to fly from Jacksonville. Our friends, Phil and Annette Ellis, who worked for Delta, would put Denise up at their home the night before each flight. Then she would fly out at six in the morning and wind up in Los Angeles by noon, west coast time. Annette's mom would pick Denise up from the airport and drive her to her appointment at the Institute in Santa Monica. Then she would usually take her home with her, cook a meal, and give her a bed for the night before taking her back to the airport early the next morning. When I think about all the people who just happened to be in the right place at the right time in order to offer the assistance we needed, I know it can't all be coincidence!

Denise was such a people person; to know her was to love her, and everyone she met knew her and her story. On her last visit to California, Annette's mom was unavailable so Denise had to go to the hotel instead. While checking in, she struck up a conversation with the attendant Marcy, as the young woman was struggling with some issues. Marcy and Denise were familiar with each other and she knew Denise had a strong faith. Marcy confided in Denise, and Denise simply told her she needed to turn her troubles over to the Lord. Marcy said she really wanted to do that but just felt like something was blocking her from doing so. Denise told her to come up to her room on her next break, and Denise would pray with her and try to help her. Denise called me from her room, feeling excited and asking me for instructions on how to pray with someone and invite them into a life with Christ. I wasn't totally sure what was proper so I got out our "Alpha" handbook, (a kind of Bible study we were involved in), and read the prayer of invitation to her from there.

When Marcy came to the room, she told Denise that she had been seeing a married man and was upset because the man would not leave his family to marry her. She knew this was not right and felt it was keeping her from a close relationship with God. Denise told her that she had no choice but to end this relationship and begin a new life in Christ that would lead her to a better way of living. She told her that what she was doing was wrong and would always bring her trouble and being with a man who could do this to his own family was not worth having anyway. She told her that Jesus was the way, the truth, and the life and she would like to pray with her. Denise asked, "Would you like to have a relationship with Jesus?"

Marcy replied, "Yes, absolutely."

Denise led her through the prayer, and for the first time,

brought another soul into a relationship with Christ. And Jesus would grant this person a new life and a better way. Denise remained in touch with Marcy over the years, and it pleased her to hear how her life changed and improved. She was forever grateful to Denise for what she had done.

Fighting Back – Battling Brain Tumors

He said I only had a year to live,
I said maybe so, but maybe not.
He said I'm a man, who's wise and learned,
Everyday I get paid for my advice.
I said that's fine but I'll remind you,
I'm stronger than your laboratory mice.
David M. Bailey, "Hey"[14]

In the summer of 1998, I had just begun a new job open-
ing some Schlotzsky's Delis for a franchisee in Gainesville
when Denise was diagnosed with her first brain tumor. I was
actually in Austin, Texas when we got the news, as I was
training for my new position. I hated not being there for
Denise when she was given the news. I finished my training early and came home as soon as possible. Found by a
routine annual brain MRI, the tumor brought reality to one
of our worst nightmares. I was certain that this would be the

way Denise would finally succumb to this awful disease. The tumor was about one centimeter in diameter and was located almost perfectly in the center of her brain. This was not an area that was easily accessible to surgery.

We made an appointment with our friend Dr. Bill Mendenhall, the bow-tie guy, and he explained to us the gravity of the situation. The only good news was that we lived in Gainesville, Florida which happened to be home of The Brain Institute, Shands Hospital of The University of Florida. The head of the institute was Dr. Bill Friedman, and Dr. Mendenhall had made us an appointment to see him. By now, Dr. Mendenhall had gotten to know us very well, and he knew that I was a man of many questions, which is sometimes irritating to doctors. He also knew that I was not concerned about irritating doctors so long as it meant my questions were answered, and I had a clear understanding of our entire situation. All I cared about was my wife, and making real sure that she was given every opportunity at the best treatment known to mankind. *What's wrong with that?* I would ask myself. Dr. Mendenhall explained to us that Dr. Friedman was a very intelligent man and that sometimes when patients asked a lot of questions a kind of imaginary wall would come down between him and the patient.

Bill Friedman was a very soft spoken, gentle man who appeared to be much younger than what I had imagined. I was careful to ask very specific questions, and he answered them in a very clear and simple way that even I could understand. I probably asked a couple of the questions more than once out of shear nervousness but Dr. Friedman was patient with me, and I appreciated that. It was obvious though that once everything was laid on the table, he was ready to move on to whatever was next on his agenda, and I didn't have a problem with that. I wasn't there to waste his time.

We learned that there was a relatively new procedure that Dr. Friedman had helped to pioneer called Stereotactic Radiosurgery. The procedure used a very fine beam of radiation that could be stopped directly on a specific end point. The beam would then be rotated on an axis in order to surround the end point with a focused beam of intense radiation thus destroying all cells and tissue at the end point. It was kind of like holding a magnifying glass between the sun and a dry leaf only imagine being able to rotate the glass and hitting the center of the leaf from all sides and directions. This procedure was found to be highly successful for many types of cancers, including melanoma. After all, this is not low-dose radiation. The other amazing thing about this procedure is that there are very little side effects and only the tissue at the end point is affected by the radiation. The worst part of the procedure is that the patient has to be saddled with a head frame that is rather brutally screwed into the person's skull; this is the only painful part of the procedure and is tolerated with valium and local anesthetic. Once the procedure is completed, the head frame is removed and the patient walks out of the hospital with a pretty good headache, some pain relievers, and the confidence of knowing their tumor is dying.

Of course, I searched the Internet for all other options, and this procedure was the only option that offered much of any hope at all. We scheduled the treatment and were anxious to get on with it. The only draw back of the treatment could be the size of the tumor; large tumors were not able to be successfully treated in this manner. Anything larger than three centimeters posed a problem, but we were fortunate that Denise's tumor was still small enough to be treated.

We went in for our treatment, and it was pretty interesting how the day was scheduled. The treatment was only given once per week, usually on a Tuesday, and people would come from all over the world to have this done. When we got there, we were introduced to a nurse, named Phil who was there to guide us through the day. He was very important to us because he was the one handing out the valium, which was much needed for the pain associated with the pain of the placement of the halo. Usually, there were about ten patients all together, and one by one, they would be lead into a room to be fitted with their head frame. They would even take a Polaroid of each patient with their head frame, and a group shot was also part of the agenda. The head frame formed a circle at about the level of the person's nose, and Denise used to joke around that this was her fallen halo.

I believe the purpose of the head frame is two-fold. One is to secure the person's head to a table so that there can be no movement whatsoever during the procedure. Second is the circular device surrounding the persons head helps with the mapping of the tumors inside the brain? The tumor or tumors are found via a three-dimensional picture using a MRI, and the head frame provides a boundary with which measurements can depict the exact location of each tumor. This is just my understanding of how this works.

A couple of weeks following the procedure, we had a problem. Denise was experiencing severe headaches and this was not supposed to happen. We scheduled a follow-up MRI and met with Dr. Friedman and his entourage. There was good news and bad news. The tumor was dying; however, it was suffering the effects of something called Necrosis, a kind of swelling and bleeding out of a dying tumor. This was taking up space in Denise's brain thus causing pressure and the severe headaches. The dying tumor could not be removed; therefore, we had to rely on a powerful steroid, decadron, to reduce the swelling in the brain. The decadron worked like a charm, but I was about to find out just how awful the side effects of steroids can be.

Denise became very compulsive, aggressive, and demanding, totally different from her natural self. She craved Oreo cookies and ate them by the bag, coincidentally gaining fifty pounds. She also couldn't sleep at night and would sometimes be up for several days at a time, cleaning and organizing the house over and over again. This behavior became extremely irritating to me and caused a great deal of stress in our marriage. I thought it would never end. We would complain to the doctors about the side effect, but they would just prescribe sleeping pills and say it was only temporary. *Easy for them to say*, I thought. *They don't have to live with the monster they created; I do.* I missed my wife and I wanted her back I would have to be patient like never before and that was not my strong suit.

Finally, one day I couldn't take it any longer, so I called Dr. Friedman on a Sunday afternoon and told him I was taking Denise off of the steroids whether he liked it or not. He told me to calm down and that we could not just stop the steroids cold turkey that could kill her.

"Great, what do we do then?" I asked. He explained that Denise would have to be weaned off of the drug, and it would take several weeks to do so, but we could start the process today. I did as he said, and we began the long process of getting Denise off of the steroids.

A few weeks later though we had another problem, Denise woke up at two in the morning with severe leg pain running through her thighs, knees, and calves She was crying and asked me to rub her legs. After an hour of rubbing her legs until they were raw, I called and woke up our friend Dr. Mendenhall. He suggested some Tylenol and perhaps hot compresses or a hot bath, and I did what he said. The only problem was that Denise could not walk so I had to carry her into the tub. That didn't work either, so I called Dr. Mendenhall again. He suggested I take her to the ER; actually I was hoping he would say that. By the time we got to the ER, it was a little after four o'clock and the doctors were able to find a bed for Denise and hook her to an IV. I was so shook up that I called our pastor, Dan Johnson, and asked him if he would come down and pray with us, and he did. They gave Denise some pain meds via the IV, and she finally went to sleep. The doctor on duty thought that perhaps the cancer had spread to the bones in Denise's legs and perhaps this was causing her the pain; now I was really upset.

This didn't really make sense to me though. *Why would the cancer travel to both legs, at exactly the same time, in exactly the same place?* Later that morning someone reached Dr. Friedman, and he told them that this could be a side effect of the steroids being taken away from Denise, and that's exactly what it was. At times, the Decadron was our best friend. At other times, it was our biggest enemy.

The doctors at John Wayne Cancer Institute were in complete agreement with our course of action, and the radio surgery was also a procedure they were experimenting with. Dr. Emmerson told me that he thought we should continue to keep Denise on the vaccine, as he did not feel that brain metastasis proved a failure of the vaccine itself. He explained to me that there was a physiological barrier called the blood-brain barrier that naturally prevented some substances from being delivered to the brain. It is very complicated, but the molecules would have to be designed small enough and in such a way as to allow them to pass through this barrier. He made it quite clear that they did not believe the vaccine treated the brain; therefore, the vaccine had not failed on Denise. In fact, there had been no metastasis to any other location in her body or no systemic disease, which was quite amazing for someone with Denise's form of aggressive melanoma. He told me we should just continue to treat Denise's brain disease separately from the rest of the body, and that's exactly what we did.

One of the most difficult parts of dealing with cancer is the constant concern of finding more cancer. Because of the brain tumor, Denise would have to be checked for more brain tumors every three months. This was the most nerve-wracking experience a person can ever have to deal with. In the movie *Gladiator*, there is a scene where the gladiator is about to be put to death and the Roman leader is raising and lowering his thumb to see what the audience would like to have happen. Then finally he either gives the thumbs up to let him live or the thumbs down for him to be finished off, that is how we feel each time we are receiving the results of an MRI.[15] I would estimate that Denise and I were in that arena roughly fifty times over the nine and a half years she was battling the cancer.

The problem with melanoma in the brain is that it usually spreads there microscopically with a splatter type effect. Microscopically means that it cannot be seen, even with an MRI until it has grown to at least one millimeter in size, which consists of thousands of cancer cells. This means that the cancer is probably going to show up in many places within the brain, in time. The good thing about the radio surgery was that it could be performed over and over again, and some people can be treated for up to fifty lesions. The bad news was that the cancer was not going to necessarily stop at fifty, and eventually you were going to run out of bullets.

Six months after her first brain tumor, Denise was diagnosed with two more tumors. Each was treated as before during a single treatment and both were killed completely. Three months later, three more tumors were discovered and were also quickly treated and taken care of. The good news was that there still was no cancer to be found systemically, and this continued to be a miracle in itself. After all, we knew the cancer was still very active as evidenced by what was happening in Denise's brain, but for some reason the cancer had not spread to any other location in Denise's body.

By this time, Denise had been battling cancer for over four years, and for her, just to be alive was a miracle, let alone to be going pretty strong and without systemic disease. But then, as I mentioned earlier, the John Wayne Cancer Institute decided that Denise was to be taken off of the vaccine. I was very upset, afraid, and really overwhelmed for the first time in a long while. There were times I wished Denise would just die and get it over with so that I didn't have to deal with this any longer. I knew in my heart that this was the only way I'd ever be done with this, unless a miracle happened and Denise was cured. The one thing I knew was that I would never stop fighting for Denise as long as she lived; it wasn't in me to give up.

But that didn't mean that I didn't want it to end; it was a terrible feeling. I remember asking our pastor, Dan Johnson, to come over to the Schlotzsky's Deli for lunch because I really needed to talk to him. He did, and I laid my feelings on the table for him and told him I thought it might be best for me if Denise simply died and we got things over with. I don't remember what he said, but I do know this. Dan prayed for me that day, and incredibly, I never felt that way again! I couldn't believe that I had ever wanted this fight to be over! I felt stronger, more confident, and was now ready to continue the quest for a cure. I can't explain it other than to believe that perhaps just unloading my feelings on my friend relieved my burdens and helped me to be more mentally prepared to go on. Or perhaps, it was something different; perhaps God heard our prayers that day and he was answering them. All I know is that I felt stronger that day, and I let Dan know just that at church following his sermon on Sunday. It was an amazing feeling and I will never forget it.

Some time prior to this I had come to know a man at church named Tom Monroe. Tom had been battling a brain tumor of a different kind called a Glioblastoma Multiforme, the most devastating type of brain tumor. Tom had also done much research, and one day he gave me a folder just full of information he had printed off of the Internet. I looked through it and did not see anything that I thought was useful because Tom's disease, although a brain tumor, was very different from what Denise was battling. However, I saved the information for future reference.

Later that year, we visited Tom at the Hospice of Gainesville as his tumor had progressed and he was dying. I got to see how a brain tumor finished the life of a person, and it wasn't something I looked forward to. Later on we visited another friend who was dying of cancer, Lou Diaz. His situation was much different, as his cancer allowed him to be alert while it slowly brought about his demise. However, the thing that struck me about Lou was his faith and the fact that he was not afraid to die. That's not something that you can fake when you know your death is immanent. Lou told us that he was ready and he knew, without a doubt, that he was going to be leaving this world and going to be with the Lord. I could just see the peace and comfort in his eyes. It was a beautiful thing, and I could only hope that Denise and I would feel that way one day as our days neared an end. What a gift that was to him and his family; it really was awesome.

One night, on my way home from Schlotzsky's, I had a very strong feeling that I needed to get home and get on the computer and do some searching. Denise's brain disease was not going to stop unless we could find something to stop it in its tracks. When I got home, I was tired as I had worked a long day and closed the restaurant, but still, I turned on the computer and went to work. I couldn't find anything at all, but I still had this strong urge to keep looking until I found something. I glanced at the piece of paper that a friend had given me at church one day and she had written the words in blue ink and in all capitals, ASK, SEEK, and KNOCK. They were words of encouragement and were from scripture saying, "Ask and it will be given to you; seek and you will find; knock and the door will be opened to you. For everyone who asks receives; he who seeks finds; and to him who knocks, the door will be opened" (Matthew 7:7–8).

The words spoke to me, and I went on searching and searching until I found some information on a drug called Temozolomide. The drug is derived from an older and well-known cancer killer called BCNU. BCNU in its form is unable to break the blood-brain barrier. The altered form of Temozolomide, called Temodar, is able to make its way into the brain! I printed out the information and saved it for future reference. Interestingly, on another late night search for answers, I was looking through the folder that Tom had given me and came across something fascinating. Tom had also come across information on Temodar; perhaps he had even tried it. He had written down a name of a local oncologist, Rob Marsh, who just happened to be Denise's oncologist also. *Hmm…I wonder if I shouldn't talk to Dr. Marsh about this drug Temodar?*

A week or so later while checking my e-mail at work, I received an e-mail from a friend telling me about a brain tumor conference coming to nearby Ft. Lauderdale. I received information like this from people from time to time, and I relied on my "feeling" as to whether I'd act on it or not. This seemed different to me, and I wanted to consider going to the conference. The conference had a very interesting format; there would be the foremost neurological specialists speaking there from all over the country. And people who were dealing with various forms of brain tumors would be invited to engage with these doctors in both a public and private setting with very little expense. *What could be better than that?* I thought. The only problem was that it was Wednesday, and the conference was on the coming Saturday and Sunday.

I called Denise to see if she had anything planned that would keep us from going and if she could make arrangements for the kids. I figured that if things fell into place then it was meant to be for us to go to the conference. Denise made one phone call, the kids were good for the weekend, and there was nothing whatsoever blocking us from going. I called and made our reservation, and that was that. We were headed to Ft. Lauderdale for the weekend. Of course, my family was from Ft. Lauderdale, and so I called my mom to let her know I needed a room for a couple of nights. She said no problem; we were all set.

When we arrived at the conference, there was a registration to go through and then we also had the opportunity to sign up for a free consultation with the doctor of our choosing. The woman I spoke with asked us our particular situation, and we told her all about the melanoma that had invaded Denise's brain. She said that the best doctor for us to talk with would be a woman by the name of Dr. Debra Heros.

I said, "Great, then let's go ahead and set things up with her."

The woman looked at her schedule and responded, "Oh no, I'm sorry. Dr. Heros is completely booked solid. I'll have to put you with someone else."

"No problem," I replied. "We are just happy to be here and feel fortunate to be able to see whoever is available." *Beggars can't be choosers*, I thought to myself. I had been learning to trust the Lord, and I reasoned that he just wanted us to meet with someone else, it must be our fate. She scheduled us with a Dr. Steven Brem, who was a very well respected doctor from the Moffit Center in Tampa, a cancer center that dealt with a lot of melanoma in trials and in research.

Before the first session, we came into the conference room to find a musician up on the stage singing some songs in the style of a Cat Stevens or a Gordon Lightfoot. He played the rhythm guitar and was wearing blue jeans, a faded tee shirt, and a bandana over his head. He was very good, and we sat down to hear him play and sing. As we listened, we realized that he was a brain tumor survivor who had turned to his music as a source of strength and comfort and used the music to witness and testify to others. He had a very strong faith, as evidenced by the lyrics of his songs and had beaten incredible odds by surviving several years battling a type of tumor known as Glioblastoma Multiforme. Most people with this diagnosis didn't last a year. This young man, David M. Bailey, had been going strong for three or four years at this time. His songs sang of hope, faith and love, the underlying message of the four gospels, but what really grabbed our attention was a song called "Hey." It was a song that was defiant to what the doctors had told him was going to happen and really hit home with Denise and I and what we had experienced with our doctors.

We sat in on the first speaker's session and listened intently to his presentation. I noticed that predominantly he was speaking about primary brain tumors, tumors that start in the brain. Mostly these are Glioblastomas and Astrocytomas, very deadly forms of malignant brain cancer. The doctor was Dr. Keith Black, a highly respected neurologist from the West Coast. He was someone I had researched and had considered traveling to speak to, now I wouldn't have to.

When he completed his presentation, we were given the opportunity to step up to a microphone and ask any questions we liked. I was a bit nervous but wasn't about to miss out on this opportunity, so I stepped in line and waited for my turn as I collected my thoughts. When my turn arrived, I described our situation with the recurring brain tumors caused by Denise's melanoma and all the treatments we had done so far. I explained that we had come to the conference searching for answers and were hoping to find a way of treating the brain for the microscopic disease that we knew was present but could not see. We had success with treating large tumors but kept having more and more tumors appearing and wanted to attack the microscopic disease also so that we could eventually cure Denise's brain. I was not prepared for his answer.

"Well, you all have certainly tried just about all the latest and most promising treatments available and have had some success, haven't you?"

"Yes sir, we have," I answered.

"I'm sorry to say that I am just disappointed that there is not something more available that could be of help to you at this time. We are working on several new approaches, but they are still a ways off from trial."

"What about the Dendretic Cell Vaccine that I've read you are working on? Isn't there a phase I trial about to begin?" I asked intently.

"Well now, the Dendretic Cell Vaccine is an interesting new approach, but I'm afraid it is still too far off in the future to be of any use to you right now, perhaps in another year of so it will be an option for you. I'm sorry," he said.

"Well thank you for your time, I appreciate all you are trying to do," I replied as I stepped away from the microphone. *That was pretty discouraging*, I thought to myself as Denise and I left the room.

We decided to go and have some lunch. As we left, a young lady whose husband was also battling brain tumors from melanoma approached me, and we compared stories and notes. We exchanged e-mail addresses and phone numbers and decided to keep in touch in case one of us ever came up with any good research that could be of use. She also had a young child at home, and I felt sorry for her, as I understood what it was like to walk in her shoes. Her husband was doing worse than Denise, and it did not sound like he had much time left to live. I could feel her desperation in the air as we spoke. Six months later, she called to tell me that her husband had died from the brain cancer, and she asked me how Denise was doing. I almost felt guilty telling her that Denise was still alive and doing pretty well. Again, I could feel her pain as we finished our conversation and I said goodbye.

When we returned to the conference center, we found David M. Bailey sitting behind his table of CD's selling his latest album. He was very quiet, but if anyone could get him to come out of his shell, it was Denise. She spoke with him for quite a while and shared some of their war stories. David used his music and lyrics to inspire others; Denise used her smile and her positive attitude. We purchased a few of David's CD's and went back inside to hear him perform before the next session. David was singing a beautiful, but sad song and I couldn't help but notice a woman a couple of rows in front of us just weeping like a baby. I could tell she was very touched by David's music.

The next session brought new hope to me, as there would be a complete panel of four or five doctors on stage with whom I would run my questions by. I thought, *Well, just because the hot-shot from California had no ideas doesn't mean one of these guys wouldn't have some answers for me.* Once they had completed their talk, which seemed to drag on forever, I was ready to rock and roll and was the first one to the microphone. Much to my dismay, each of them were stumped by my questions also. The only comfort I had was in knowing that we had been doing every possible thing known to mankind and had left no stone unturned. I guess I just couldn't believe I had been that thorough; surely someone had to have something that we could at least try!

I just know that there is some reason God had brought us here to this conference, I pondered. As we walked out of the room with our heads hanging low, a woman followed us out the door and tapped me on the shoulder.

"Excuse me sir, I just couldn't help but hear your questions and noticed that the doctors were of little to no help to you," she said softly. I noticed that it was the same woman who had been crying earlier.

"Yes, ma'am," I replied, "they haven't been of much help, but we'll just keep on searching." Just then, I noticed her nametag, Dr. Debra Heros.

"Well, I am a doctor and would like to share some information with you and your wife that may be of help to you if you have the time," she said.

I was a bit stunned and said, "Oh, wow, you are Debra Heros we had been told we should consult with you, but you were totally booked solid. We would love to speak with you, just name the time and place."

"How about five o'clock in the Seaside conference room later today," she asked.

"That's perfect, we'll be there," I said excitedly.

Before our meeting with Dr. Heros, we had our free consultation with a Dr. Steven Brem of the Moffit Center in Tampa. We had heard nothing but good things about the Moffit Center, and I had spoken with several of the melanoma researchers there in the past. It was so near to Gainesville and a logical choice of a place to go for treatment, but for one reason or another, they just never had any trials that we could get into. This meeting would not prove any different. Dr. Brem was friendly enough. However, he had absolutely nothing to offer, and we were not surprised. After all, he was one of the doctors on the panel that I had previously pleaded our case to. At least now I knew that this door was tightly shut. We left and came back for our meeting with Dr. Heros and spent over an hour talking to her. She was a very compassionate woman and was a very highly respected doctor who worked out of Jackson Memorial Hospital in Miami. Her husband was also a very well respected oncologist there. She had been working very closely with a Dr. Jose' Lutzky who is the Director of the Melanoma Multidisciplinary Program at Mt. Sinai Cancer Center in Miami Beach. He had been doing some experimentation with two drugs that had shown synergy when used simultaneously.

The first drug was none other than Temozolomide, otherwise called Temodar. It is the cancer drug I spoke about earlier, BCNU that is altered to make it receivable by the brain. The other drug was an old, old drug called Thalidomide. Thalidomide had been prescribed in the 1970's for another use and was infamous for causing devastating birth defects in babies that prevented the development of their upper and lower extremities. Now, scientists had considered those effects and how they might affect a cancer cell. What happened to the babies was that the blood supply was being cut of to the development of normal cells thus stunting the growth of the child's arms and legs, the process is known as anti-angiogenesis. If this drug is given to a patient, the theory is that the blood supply would be cut off to all of the person's cells, including any cancer cells causing death to all cells, which is what chemotherapy does. However, the body is always reproducing normal cells so the only cells permanently destroyed would be the cancer cells. Couple this with the effects of the Temodar making its way to the brain killing any microscopic disease and viola, no more brain disease! It made sense to me and the beauty was that the side effects would be very minimal. Thalidomide generally makes the patient tired in high doses and could cause some neuropathy (tingling and minor damage to some nerve endings). The Temodar would be taken in a very low dose but over the long term would have similar effects of typical chemotherapy, lower blood levels and weakness to the immune system causing the patient to be more prone to other illnesses. However, these are side effects brought about by long-term use. At this stage in the game, we were just hoping to stay alive in the short term, so long-term problems would actually be a blessing of sorts.

Dr. Heros wrote down everything we needed to know so we could explain the therapy to Dr. Marsh, Denise's oncologist in Gainesville. He could call either her or Dr. Lutzky if he had any questions or concerns, so we assumed that there would be no problem in getting this therapy started right there in good old Gainesville. That way our local oncologist would be right on top of things in order to monitor our progress.

We thanked Dr. Heros profusely and thought it was no coincidence that her name was Heros, she was our hero, that's for sure. We went there to listen to doctors from all over the country and not a single one of them were worth one bit of use to us. Then sitting there in the audience just happens to be this extremely compassionate doctor who is willing to put her neck on the line for us and give us her precious time so that we may have hope! There was only one logical explanation for what happened to us that weekend in

Miami—God was leading us and directing others to our aid. It is just that simple.

Many things had to happen in order for us to be sitting at a table with Debra Heros, and it is no coincidence that I had been directed earlier to find information on the new drug Temozolomide. God is good, God is alive, and God cares about us and loves us so much that he was directly involved in our battle against cancer.

Seeing God

I caught a glimpse of your splendor
In the corner of my eye
The most beautiful thing I've ever seen
And it was like a flash of lightning
Reflected off the sky
And I know I'll never be the same
Third Day, "Show Me Your Glory"[16]

The difficult thing about faith is that God is somewhat invisible to us. We are constantly looking for proof of his existence and wondering why he won't just materialize, much the way Jesus did, and show us his face. In addition, I believe you actually have to believe, before you will be able to see him, kind of a catch twenty-two for some of us. I don't think any of us will ever actually see God the way we would like to or imagine. I think the best we can hope for is to see what he is doing in our lives around us and then just knowing that he is there is sufficient.

In my faith journey, once I actually believed and began to trust in God and his very existence, I began to see some of the things that he had done for me. In the early part of my journey, I began to look back at things that had occurred weeks, months, or even years before and finally recognized where God had been involved and made something happen. It isn't a magic trick or a miracle really, because God works through the Holy Spirit that he sends to be inside of each believer. Then what occurs is, people with the Spirit act on what they feel or hear God asking them to do. Much of the time you think it is just an every day normal happening and other times it is just so incredible you know that it just had to be from the Lord.

Before Denise became diagnosed with cancer, probably just a couple of months prior, a friend of mine, Keith Lerner, called to tell me he thought it would be a good idea to take another look at the life insurance I was carrying. I was reluctant because people were always trying to sell me more and more of what I didn't need. *Besides*, I thought, *he is not my insurance agent; he is a good customer of mine and a friend.* After some thought, I decided, Denise was pregnant with my son and maybe it would make sense to have some more coverage. If my agent wanted to take care of me then perhaps he should have been more aware of the changes taking place in my life and called me himself. All the life insurance I owned on Denise at the time was a whole life policy with a fifty thousand dollar death benefit so I definitely was not over-insured. What my friend and I decided to do was to purchase a term life policy with a death benefit of one hundred thousand dollars. Term insurance is very inexpensive, especially on young people, so I felt good that if anything happened to Denise I would have a decent chunk of change coming my way to help pay the bills and provide childcare for Raechel and Richard. What I did not realize was the way that God would use these death benefits for a different purpose altogether.

A year after Denise began the vaccine trial she suffered a setback. The doctors at John Wayne found three new lymph nodes containing melanoma. Denise was devastated and so was I. The only good that came from it was that this new setback caused the viatical company to give a much higher percentage on my remaining life insurance policy. The bad news was that now her prognosis was much worse, and the expectation was that this was just the beginning of the bad news. This only caused us to want to live and live well that much more.

We decided to cash in the policy for eighty percent of value and put the money into a house on the outskirts of town. Denise was so happy and excited. There was no question that we had made the right decision. The house sat on the edge of a couple of hundred of undeveloped acres, and we had countless hours of walks in the woods and quiet times on the porch. We made friends with many of the neighbors; the neighborhood was perfect for a young family. Halloween became one of our favorite holidays, as a great neighborhood can really make that night such a good time. We bought a yellow lab and a cat. Life was good! The kids and Denise would sit in the driveway, playing with sidewalk chalk and drawing hopscotch on the pavement. It always made me smile when I'd come home and see all the writing on the concrete by the garage or in the street. A few years later, when I got lucky in the stock market, Denise forced me into adding a pool with a slide. *What a great thing that was; I'm so glad that I listened to her*. Denise, the kids and I spent hours and hours in that pool just playing games and having fun. Denise was all about making memories, and I have her to thank for all the good ones. Denise and I were so thankful that God could take a terrible situation and turn it into such a huge blessing.

Looking back, I think God orchestrated the whole opportunity by having Keith Lerner talk me into buying that second policy. If not for that, who knows what might have been. This is a good example of God working in my life without me suspecting a thing. It wasn't until some time later that I was able to recognize exactly what had happened and who was responsible.

What if all the positive thoughts and energy brought on by these good times really did help to extend Denise's life? What if we didn't have these good times to look back on today, what a tragedy that would be? Suppose I had decided that the death benefit had been more important to use in the event of her death, rather than using the money to help fund a life worth living. I promised myself one thing when Denise came home on that fate-filled day of her diagnosis—no matter what happened, I did not want to ever look back and regret anything I did helping Denise fight her disease. Gladly, I can honestly say, I have none.

Something happened twice in our Gainesville home that Denise and I rarely spoke of. On both occasions, it was in the middle of the day, and we were sitting alone together in our living room. It was as if a flash of lightening had flashed before our eyes in a split second. When it happened, Denise and I just looked at each other bewildered and confused. We both knew immediately that we had experienced something of divine nature.

"Did you see that," I said right as it happened.

"What was that?" Denise asked.

"It was like lightening, but there is no storm or clouds outside. Perhaps it was electricity jumping out of the sockets, like a power surge or something."

"This may sound crazy, Rod, but I think it was from God, like angels passing through us or something." As crazy as she sounded, I thought it made perfect sense, and I was actually thinking the same thing but had been afraid to say so. The light was so bright, but it did not blind our eyes like a reflection of the sun or a bolt of lightening would do. The second time it happened, months later, we just asked each other if the other had seen it then smiled, as we simply felt blessed by a divine presence. We just accepted that God wanted to give us a glimpse of his glory and we were thankful that he did.

There are many ways in which we can chose to see God. Perhaps it can be in the physical sense such as what happened to Denise and me in our living room. More often than not, however, it is a choice we make in seeing all he does for us through others and by his Holy Spirit and through answered prayers. For example, on the day of Denise's memorial service in Gainesville I had asked God to give me incredible strength and presence of mind to help me to make it through the day. Not only did I want to be strong so I could honor Denise and tell others what a wonderful wife and mother she was to our family, but I mostly wanted to let everyone know that God was real and awesome. That he had never let us down. That Denise's death was not a failure by any means whatsoever. In fact, just the opposite was true. Her life was a success and a miracle that God had provided for us. That without him, her life would have ended six months after her diagnosis, just as the doctors had predicted and seen happen so many times before. Instead, with him, her life lasted nine and one half years after diagnosis, something that was practically unprecedented and impossible by any standard.

On that, day I felt stronger and more confident than on any day I can remember. I was able to stand before the five hundred people and witness to each of them what God had done for Denise and our family. I made my point by telling the crowd, "You probably are wondering how I could have the strength stand before you and speak to you today on what should be the saddest day of my life." They seemed to nod in agreement with me. Then I asked them, "How many of you have been praying for me and asking God to give me peace and strength at this most difficult time?" And all of them raised their hands simultaneously. "Then we should not be surprised that I have peace and strength because God does answer our prayers, and he has answered your prayers here today." We can see God anytime we want to, all we have to do is open our eyes and chose to do so.

Richard and Holly Schackow used to eat in my little Italian restaurant quite frequently. I still remember how they would order a small vegetarian pizza and share it with each other.

They were always very sweet and pleasant to be with, just two of the kindest people anyone would ever want to know.

When Denise and I joined Trinity United Methodist Church shortly after her diagnosis, we came to know the Schackows even better. Richard and Holly were no strangers to difficult times, as Richard suffered from epilepsy, which caused him to suffer severe seizures on a regular basis. Holly had also been through her own personal struggles . There was some common ground here between the four of us, and it caused us to become closer to each other. People who suffer together, persevere together, and grow closer to God together. When that happens, they begin to pray together, and when they pray together, things happen.

Holly is the friend who gave me the words Ask, Seek and Knock that I taped to my computer for inspiration. One day after Denise had died, I saw those words looking at me, and I truly felt like God was telling me I needed to give Holly a call. When I did, she broke down into tears and told me that I could never know how much it meant to her to hear from me right at the moment I called.

She explained that she had been really, really struggling and had been thinking of her old friend Denise just as I called. Denise was always a very strong source of support for her, and she was really missing her just at that moment. It always amazes me at how God can make something like that happen. I think we need to see God at work from time to time just to help us keep our faith alive. Sometimes it will be at a low moment in our lives or an unexpected way that he uses us to help someone at their time of need. There are many events that have occurred in my life that my mind will forever forget; these events, however, will not be among them.

There were many times throughout this ordeal that I was able to see God at work. Many of them I have already mentioned earlier in this story. There was the man I met at Ayers Medical Center who told me to lay my hands on Denise as she lay sleeping and pray for God to perform his miracles on her. There was the mother-in-law of my friend Pete Minor who gave me a vile of oil to anoint Denise with on her forehead and to pray for God's divine intervention. The acts of these two individuals encouraged me to take action, action that required faith! These were critical steps that had to be taken so that I could grow in my faith and truly believe. There is no way of knowing what doors may not have been opened had these steps not been taken. I have to mention again the time that Dan Johnson ran into Denise at the Atlanta International Airport on her return trip from L.A. after she had been given some bad news. What were the odds of that happening? If a person could not see God working right there then I suppose they would have to be completely blind. And Dan certainly put his faith immediately into action by anointing Denise in the middle of the airport and Denise did the same by accepting his offer of faith. There are so many people out there who claim to be Christian and never take leaps of faith like this for fear of being foolish or looking silly. Ironically, it is truly foolish not to take these simple steps and I don't believe a person will ever really see God without doing so.

Another way that I truly saw God was in the number of high quality friends that surrounded Denise and I. God had completely covered us with the most wonderful caring people we could ever hope to meet, let alone have them as our friends. I remember one time at Trinity we were invited to a healing service in a small quiet room on the church campus. When we entered the room we could actually "feel" the love so deeply that it moved me to tears without anyone having said a word, it was truly overwhelming. I think that if God could ever be manifested in a physical form and I could actually be standing in his presence, that is how it would feel only probably even more intensely.

Friends were always checking on us and visiting with us. They were always there whenever there was another MRI, treatment, surgery, test, or whatever. How comforting it was to see them whenever there was another hurdle to cross. When Denise was about to go into surgery, not just any surgery but brain surgery, there was always several of us in the prep room huddled around Denise. We used to have to sneak everyone back there because we were really only allowed to have one or two visitors at a time. After a while, there would be five or six of us there, and we would be telling jokes, laughing, praying, and crying all at once. Denise always had a way of putting us all at ease, *imagine that*. We never could have made it through all we had to endure without our friends. They were there with us all the way up until the bitter end.

Whatever you do in life, don't ever forget to give God the credit he is due. Just look back on your life and remember all that you have asked of him, and you will be amazed at all the times he delivered for you. Once you have done this, you will begin to expect it, and you will sometimes see him working in real time. Or perhaps it will be just minutes or seconds after he has done something for you and you will say, "Yep there he is again. Thank you, Lord!" *What a wonderful feeling it is*!

Expanding Territory

Jabez's Prayer

"Jabez cried out to the God of Israel, 'Oh that you would bless me and enlarge my territory! Let your hand be with me, and keep me from harm so that I will be free from pain.' And God granted his request."

1 Chronicles 4:10

Like many churches, our church in Gainesville spent a lot of time studying and preaching on the Prayer of Jabez. There were several books and study guides published on the prayer that circled the country like a wild fire back in 2001 or 2002. I'm sure Denise and I prayed this prayer many, many times, and I believe our prayers were answered. I suppose that for the purpose of sharing our story with others in a different area and perhaps having a profound effect on their lives and their relationships with God it was a good thing but that is not to say it made our lives better or any easier.

About that time, I was really struggling with the company I worked for. We had opened four Schlotzsky's Delis, two in Gainesville and two in Tallahassee, and we were finding it increasingly difficult to make ends meet. We had been talking about beginning a new concept, and we all would supposedly have an opportunity to have some ownership in the new venture along with some say as to what particular concept we would chose. *So much for that*. A sports bar was chosen, and I really did not wish to be in the bar business, especially in a college town. Excessive drinking and irresponsibility had cost me my college education, and I simply did not want to contribute to other young people making the same mistakes I had made. I decided that it was time for me to make a career move.

An old friend presented an interesting opportunity to me that I thought could really be a winner. It was a restaurant for sale called Cracklin' Jacks that had a very interesting concept selling the tastes of old Florida: catfish, fried chicken, baby back ribs, frog legs, gator tail, and the usual variety of steaks and seafood. There were only two potential problems—the place was a complete dump, and it was located several hundred miles to the south in Naples, Florida. Now, fixing it up would be easy and only help to increase the revenues, so that was a no-brainer. However, moving my wife and kids away from their comfort zone in Gainesville would require a great deal of prayer and consideration.

Denise had established a huge support structure in Gainesville, from pastors to doctors and a plethora of very close friends. On the surface, it would seem that the decision would be simple—*don't even consider it*. However, Denise had been cruising along without many difficulties for almost an entire year now. In addition, there just weren't any real attractive opportunities I could see in Gainesville. I had allowed cancer to rule my life for the better part of eight years, and I was growing tired of it. Every decision I made seemed to revolve around what was happening concerning Denise's health or what I was afraid was going to happen at some point in the future. I also needed to consider the long-term outlook. I really felt I needed to find an opportunity that could provide us with the potential for a good, long-term income. If something did happen to Denise then we would be completely reliant on my sole income. I wanted to afford a private Christian education for Raechel and Richard, and one day there would also be college to think about.

In any event, I decided to take the opportunity and move the concept back to Gainesville so Denise and the kids would not have to move. I planned to commute on weekends while I learned the concept and took on a partner that would manage the Naples operation. Unfortunately, the partnership failed after several months, and we were forced to make a permanent move to Naples anyway. It was one of the most difficult things I ever had to ask my wife to do, and rarely a day goes by that I wonder what would have been had we all just stayed in good old Gainesville. In any event, our prayers were answered, like it or not and our territory was expanded.

As luck would have it, Denise was diagnosed with another brain tumor just a few weeks after buying out my partner and making the decision to move permanently to Naples. Fortunately, I had not sold the house yet, so we decided that Denise and the kids would stay the summer of 2003 in Gainesville while receiving treatment. Toward the end of the summer and just before the start of the school year, Denise and I rented a house on the Isle of Capri near Marco Island. It was a nice house located right on the water and just a few miles from Cracklin' Jacks. There was a church just walking distance from the house called Capri Christian Church pastored by Curt Ayers and his lovely wife Dreama. Before Denise and the kids moved down, I visited the church and went to speak to Curt about my situation. I was feeling really lousy about being away from home while Denise was battling brain tumors. I couldn't understand why God allowed me to move so far away from home while Denise was having recurrences.

I had prayed and prayed about moving, and I always had peace with my decision up until that point. When I asked Dan about it, he simply asked me, "Did you pray about your decision to move, Rod?"

"Yes I did," I replied.

"And what did you hear God saying to you?" he asked.

"I distinctly heard him say it was fine and that he would be with me wherever I was."

"So, do you think God made a mistake then, Rod?" He asked. There was no need to answer; I got the point.

One Sunday during service, Curt told the congregation that he would be available to speak to anyone who might want to talk to him shortly after service. It seemed that he was looking directly at me when he said it. I suppose he could see it in my eyes how troubled I was, so I took him up on his offer. I told him how difficult it was to be away from my family during such a crucial time. To my amazement, Curt told me that he knew how I felt because he had a very young son die from a brain tumor roughly a year earlier! *How comforting it was to be talking to someone who could truly relate to my problems.*

Curt was very clear on his advice to me. "Rod, it really doesn't matter what happened in the past or how you got to this point in time. You made the decisions you made with the best of intentions for your family and that is all that really matters. What you have to focus on is what happens from this point forward, and God will be right there with you for whatever will come." I came away from that meeting with a renewed spirit and understanding and felt like God was putting people in my path that would help me to get through whatever came next. Nothing is ever more comforting than that.

Early in the summer of 2003, we had hoped to move Denise and the kids down to the Isle of Capri where I was renting a house from Judy Spates (the woman who had helped us so much when we had to travel to Maryland when Denise was first diagnosed). Unfortunately, Denise's cancer had other ideas. It seemed a new brain tumor had appeared, and it was larger than any other we had dealt with in the past. We visited with Dr. Friedman in Gainesville, and he told us that because of the size of the tumor, Radiosurgery would not be an option, as we had done so many times in the past. This time Denise would have to undergo brain surgery. Our hearts were broken.

However, Denise was such a trooper; she refused to let it get her down. She decided that she was thankful the tumor could be removed without much risk of serious side effects, and so the sooner they could perform the surgery the better.

Within a few days, the surgery was successfully performed, and Denise was out of the hospital. Incredibly, she only spent two days in recovery and was completely upbeat throughout the entire ordeal. As usual, our friends in Gainesville were extremely supportive and astounded by Denise and her incredible spirit. Before the year was out, Denise had to have two additional brain surgeries for two more tumors that were too large for Radiosurgery. During that six-month period, Denise had also become well known to members of our new church on the Isle of Capri, as well as my sister Dottie Scofield's church, First Baptist Church of Naples. Denise had begun attending a bible study there called "Refresh-her" taught by Pastor Hayes Wicker's wife, Janet.

Before long, Denise was well known by not only all of the members of both of these well established churches but also by many of the employees and customers of Cracklin' Jacks. Denise had spent many hours working in the tiny restaurant. She often wore a cute little white hat to hide her short hair and scars while seating customers and bussing tables. Sometimes our daughter Raechel would come in and help her while she was working. It was simply precious and awe inspiring to me. Denise's incredible spirit was now being felt throughout the Naples area and literally hundreds, perhaps even thousands, of people were being touched by her and by what they could see God was doing through her. Our territory had been officially enlarged, and God was with us!

Troubled Waters

I can't stop the rain
From falling down on you again
I can't stop the rain
But I will hold you 'til it goes away
Third Day, "When the Rain Comes"[17]

While everyone else was watching in amazement, I was going through a particularly difficult time. Sure, Denise had continued to beat terrible odds and seemingly thrived under the worst of conditions, but I knew the truth. Dr. Friedman had extremely good bedside manners. He would never make predictions or tell a patient what he felt their chances were unless they really pinned him down and asked him point blank. Denise never asked those kinds of questions; I don't think she really wanted to know.

She had already beaten all the odds and proven all the experts wrong, so she figured they didn't really know what was going to happen anyway. She left those things up to God and was convinced that living her life one day at a time was the only real way to live life to the fullest. I felt like I wanted to know what was going to happen as much as possible so that I could plan accordingly, and this was an incredible burden for me. Not knowing what was coming was a luxury I did not feel I could afford. It seemed almost irresponsible to me, not for Denise but for me. I was the father and the head of household, and this was my responsibility to the family.

On one of my visits with Dr. Friedman, I asked him for a few minutes of his time in private. I asked him what he thought about our current situation and his thoughts on Denise's chances for continued survival. I was convinced that these were the most difficult questions a husband could ever have to ask. Dr. Friedman was extremely candid, calm, and frank with me. "As you know, Rod, we have been treating Denise for several years now using Radiosurgery with a great deal of success. I always felt like we had some hope for a cure for Denise by treating her in this manner. Now I feel like everything has changed. Her tumors are now coming more frequently and are much larger than they were in the past. As you are well aware, we never had to perform brain surgery during all of this time. I do not think that we can measure the time that Denise has left in terms of years but rather in months."

I thanked Bill for his brutal honesty, as the tears began to run down both of my cheeks and I shook his hand. I asked him how do I handle telling this to Denise or should I even approach her with it. He told me that he never answered any questions that were not specifically asked. He advised me to only tell Denise what she wanted to know and the only way to do that was to answer any questions she had. If she didn't ask then she didn't want or need to know; it was that simple. That was incredibly good and wise advice; he is a wonderful man and doctor. Denise would, however, prove him wrong, as she lived another fifteen months past that day.

That summer Denise had to go through a total of three brain surgeries. Twice to remove tumors and a third time to relieve the bleeding and edema from the second surgery. It was a horrific summer, all in all, but Denise never complained or let herself get down. She recovered each time with the true spirit of a champion and amazed all of us who knew her, especially me.

Following her second surgery, we had a particularly difficult time. Denise was having severe headaches that were so excruciating at one point she asked me to just shoot her and get it over with. I knew she had to be in extreme pain because she never had acted this way before. We decided to drive both vans to Gainesville to see Dr. Friedman and loaded up the dog, Lucky, our seventy-five pound yellow lab, and both kids into the Dodge caravan, while Denise drove the Toyota.

We wanted to have both cars available because we knew Denise would probably have to stay a while, and I would have to return for work once she was treated. Her pain was so bad that she was having trouble driving, and we had used all her pain meds just before we left town. We thought we could handle everything until we made it to Gainesville, four hours to our north. An hour from home I had to pull over to make sure Denise was okay because she was having trouble staying in her own lane and was feeling sick to her stomach. We had overdosed her with ibuprofen, and things just kept getting worse.

We contemplated just leaving the van on the side of the

road and then decided to give it another try. I kept the kids and the dog in my vehicle out of fear Denise would have an accident, I had really made some bad decisions that day and wasn't sure what to do next. Roughly thirty minutes up the road, I saw smoke coming from the Toyota, and Denise had to pull over to the shoulder of I-75. Incredibly the Toyota, our newest, and supposedly our most reliable, minivan had blown the engine!

So there we were, sitting on the edge of I-75 in ninety-degree heat at noon in Venice, Florida. I thought, *If this is not a complete nightmare then I don't know what one is.* Denise was suffering tremendous pain from either a new brain tumor or side effects of her earlier surgery; we had a dog and two young children with us and now had to load all our belongings into the old Dodge van with no working air conditioning. I drove to the next exit and called a local mechanic who could retrieve the Toyota for me and work on it while we were gone. I tried to make Denise as comfortable as possible and hurried the rest of the way to Gainesville. We took her directly to Shands Hospital, where they admitted her and gave her the medications necessary to make her comfortable. I had a friend meet us at our house, which still wasn't sold, to watch the children and Lucky. Much of that afternoon remains a blur to me.

The next morning Denise's scan results were in, and we were meeting with Dr. Friedman to discuss the results and put together a game plan for our latest treatment. Apparently, her previous surgery had caused significant bleeding and swelling, and this was putting a lot of pressure on Denise's brain and causing the excruciating pain Denise was feeling.

Surgery would be necessary to relieve the pressure and was scheduled for first thing the next morning; our nightmare was almost complete.

A few minutes later, the mechanic in Venice called to give me some more bad news. "Hello, Mr. Ellis, this is Vince from All-star Auto Repair. How are you this morning?"

"What can I do for you, Vince," I responded without even attempting to answer his question.

"Well, I'm afraid I have some bad news for you, sir. Are you sitting down?" he asked.

"Sure am Vince, lay it on me."

"I'm afraid the engine is blown on your van; these Cienna vans are notorious for doing this even with regular oil changes. We can replace the engine for you, but it is going to cost roughly sixty-nine hundred dollars!"

"I'll tell you what, Vince, first of all, that is a distant second place for bad news I've received this morning, and it's still early. Secondly, I'll call you later and let you know what we are going to do about it, okay?" I really couldn't care less about the stupid van; it is at times like these that you learn about the really meaningful things in life, and cars aren't one of them, unless you are stranded on I-75 without at least one working car.

Just then, it occurred to me, *What if we had decided to take just one vehicle or had abandoned the Dodge on the side of the road when Denise was driving erratically from the pain and nausea? What if we had been stranded with that Toyota van and had to wait for someone to come and get us? What if we weren't able to complete our road trip to Gainesville and Denise had to see someone at a nearby hospital? Isn't it possible that my poor decisions weren't so poor after all? Isn't it possible that a higher power was controlling our destiny?* Because of her poor condition, perhaps Denise would have caused an accident had the van continued to run? Maybe Denise would have suffered for much longer or worse—*what if we had decided to just take the Toyota and leave the Dodge at home?* I think these are reasonable questions that I will probably never know the answers to.

I had been through way too much to ever second guess the things that God can and does do for those who love Him. I know exactly what happened that day, why they happened, and who made them happen. And I know that after all was said and done, we were home in Gainesville, Denise was made comfortable, and she received the exact treatment she needed to get her well and allow her to live and enjoy another day with her family and friends. It was nothing short of a miracle, and we were not upset about the ordeal, worried about the van, or disappointed about anything. We were thankful! After her third and final surgery, we went to the hair salon together and received matching buzz-cuts. I felt it was the least I could do to show my support, and we had a few good laughs over it.

As if we didn't have enough to be concerned about, on one of our final visits to Dr. Friedman I learned of a small spot on Denise's liver that was vaguely visible on one of her routine full-body scans. This was particularly upsetting to me because I always felt that Denise should not have been taken off the vaccine she participated in at the John Wayne Cancer Institute. I specifically remembered Dr Emerson telling me that even if Denise were taken off the vaccine that the residual effects would probably last roughly thirty months.

Incredibly, it had been almost thirty months to the day

since they had callously removed Denise from their program. When discussing the liver tumor with Dr. Friedman, I told him that I felt like the John Wayne Cancer Institute performed a disservice to Denise by removing her from their trial, and I was interested in his professional opinion on the matter. Sometimes, medical professionals make an effort to protect each other, as if they are part of a fraternity or brotherhood or something, so I wasn't really sure what he would say. It was somewhat gratifying to hear him tell me that he agreed with me and wished they had kept her on their protocol. He believed, as I did, that they did not think she would live very long with brain tumors and preferred that she not be on their study when she died. The vaccine was protecting her body from metastasis all of this time, and now it had finally worn off and had left her immune system defenseless against a ruthless and unrelenting adversary. *Why did they do that?*

In any event, once we returned to Naples, we had to find a new oncologist who could help us to deal with any metastatic disease that would occur outside of Denise's brain. We were referred to a Dr. Mark Moscowicz, a quiet, sweet man with an incredible sense of humor, who Denise and I grew to love. Mark was very compassionate and levelheaded, my only complaint was that he did not seem to be as aggressive as I would prefer. However, that was only because he was a realist, and what I did not understand at the time was that part of his job was to protect his patients from themselves—or even from the people who loved them the most.

It is easy to become over-zealous during treatment, and many people are willing to put themselves or their loved ones through unnecessary suffering and trauma simply to have a glimmer of hope to keep on living. What frequently happens is living like that is not living at all.

That was where Mark and I would sometimes have a bit of an adversarial relationship, but all in all it was good because it brought balance to our regimen of treatment. As I explained to Mark on more that one occasion, Denise was not his typical patient. She was very, very special. One cannot accomplish what Denise accomplished without being special, or blessed as we preferred to think of it. I don't think it took Mark long to figure that out however. After all, Denise had survived nine years after a six-month survival prediction from Melanoma experts. She had also withstood the successful treatment of nearly thirty brain tumors. This was predominantly unheard of.

Unfortunately, chemotherapy was largely unsuccessful against Melanoma, and that was the weapon of choice that Dr. Moscowicz and all oncologists used to fight cancer. So, after some time, we were referred, at my request, to a liver specialist at the Naples Community Hospital . We were scheduled to meet a Dr. Adam Groper there, and so we did, with all of my latest research printed off the Internet neatly in my little red folder.

Dr. Groper was relatively young, maybe in his late thirties or early forties, and I really liked him. He was very honest and open to us and seemed to be willing to listen to any ideas I might have as a means to treat Denise's tumor. I really appreciated that. Most doctors I had come in contact with were basically know-it-alls and were not much interested in anything a patient advocate had to say. They probably felt like they had already heard it all and didn't want to waste their valuable time listening to a restaurant operator who was attempting to practice medicine—something they studied years and years.

Dr. Groper reviewed Denise's scans with us, and we *all* talked about the size and location of the tumor and what some of our options might be. Dr. Groper basically mentioned surgery as our only option but did not know if that would be wise due to the probability that more tumors would probably occur. That was when I reached into my folder and asked him if he had any knowledge or experience with a procedure known as Radiofrequency Ablation. Surprisingly, he said that he and his partner have a good bit of experience with the procedure and that it may, in fact, be a viable option for Denise. The procedure was much less invasive than surgery and could be repeated, if necessary, with minimal recovery time and side effects!

I was a little stunned by his response since he had not mentioned it as an option until I brought it up. I had thought for sure my idea would be shot down. Surprisingly, however, it was embraced instead, and we actually used the procedure on two occasions, once successfully on the first liver tumor and again on a second tumor. Unfortunately, however, more tumors began to appear, and we needed to try something else that might treat the entire liver, something that would treat large tumors, small tumors, and even microscopic cancer cells that had yet to be detected.

I spoke to Dr. Groper about trying chemo embolization on Denise, and he was all for it. We scheduled her for the procedure, and he was prepared to treat her liver with primarily Cisplatin, an old cancer-fighting agent that was useful against a large array of different types of cancer, melanoma primarily not being one of them. Wanting to make sure we were using the latest techniques for Denise's situation, I continued to research the Internet about different types on chemotherapy or immunotherapy being used to battle primarily liver metastasis from melanoma when I discovered some new information coming from the Thomas Jefferson University. A new study there had shown that a new approach called immunoembolization was more effective than chemoembolization. This approach used so-called cytokines instead of chemotherapy drugs, in the immunoembolization treatment of the patients. Cytokines have been reported to stimulate or modulate immune responses. The cytokines that have been used for immunoembolization at Thomas Jeferson University Hospital included GM-CSF, Interleukin 2 and interferon alpha.[18]

I thought that I should share this with Dr. Groper and make sure that we were moving forward with the best possible treatment for Denise. I called him and left a message but did not hear back from him right away. The day before her scheduled treatment, we finally made contact, and he decided to postpone her procedure until he had a chance to review the study and possibly talk with one of the lead investigators on the study. I had actually spoken with Dr. Adams to get his opinion of the study. He had moved from Thomas Jefferson University to Emory University in Atlanta and was experiencing some success with immunoembolization and so I gave the information to Dr. Groper so that he could consult with him himself.

Surprisingly, Dr. Groper agreed with this new form of

embolization, and Denise was treated accordingly. Soon, her liver disease was stabilized. We never had another issue with Denise's liver cancer, Denise took all of this just as she had taken all of her treatments, in full stride. She remained positive and hopeful all the while, and her recovery periods were always less than expected. Her doctors and nurses continued to be in complete awe of her faith, courage, and positive spirit. Denise witnessed the love of Christ to all of them and to anyone else who was nearby that was willing to listen.

Although we had achieved some success with Denise's liver disease and were somewhat stable with her brain tumors, her disease progressed and could now be seen and felt just under her skin. When I rubbed her back, I could feel the tumors growing and one large bump also appeared over her left eye. This was particularly disturbing because up until now at least we did not have to "see" or "feel" the cancer. There were actually times that we could enjoy being together and perhaps for a moment or two we could even forget that the cancer was there. That luxury was now going to disappear. The only option I knew of that offered even a remote chance of a cure for Denise was a treatment known as Interleukin Two or IL2. The problem with this option is that it is extremely toxic and requires a two-week stay in the ICU of the local hospital. The treatment itself could be fatal and the patient's vital signs had to be monitored twenty-four hours a day. The side effects were extreme flu-like symptoms including a spiking high fever, nausea, vomiting, low blood pressure, malaise, and the worst case of the chills a person could ever have. Other than that, it is a piece of cake.

Dr. Moscowicz was reluctant to put Denise through this, and on hindsight, I'm sorry I pressed so hard to put her through it myself. The problem was the unknown and the what-ifs we would have to face if we decided against it. It was after all, our last hope, and we didn't want to come this far without having given Denise every chance at survival. We did not want to live with the thought of having to ask ourselves what if we had done this or tried that. It was quite a dilemma to say the least.

Still after some serious thought, we went ahead and did the procedure. As expected, it was very tough on Denise (many people fail to even complete the treatment). Naturally, Denise did complete it, however, and once again, her staff of nurses and doctors were quite impressed with Denise's positive outlook and spirit. Their hearts were forever changed by what they experienced there with Denise. God was always on the forefront of Denise's heart and mind, and he was always there to see her through every difficulty she had to face.

Shortly after her treatment, it was quite obvious that the treatment had failed completely. There was no noticeable difference in any of her tumors. A second dose was typical for this protocol, but we could not see any reason why we should put Denise through this torture again. Perhaps, if we had seen some noticeable difference, we would have gone through the second dose for hope of a complete response. To make matters worse, a blood vessel had burst in Denise's eye, and while we were told the blood would eventually be absorbed and disappear completely, it never did. Whenever I looked my wife in the eye, it was like the cancer was staring back at me, taunting me as if to say, "How do you like me now?" I had never hated anything with all my heart the way I hate cancer. It was truly a miserable disease that showed no mercy ever, not even once!

Faith and Courage

And like a lamp on a hill Lord I pray in your will
To reveal all of you that I can.
So turn on the light and reveal all the glory.
I am not afraid.
To bear all my weakness, knowing in meekness,
I have a kingdom to gain.
Jennifer Knapp, "Martyrs and Thieves"[19]

On a subsequent visit to Dr. Moscowicz, Denise revealed that she was no longer willing to continue with the fight against her disease, at least in the medical sense. She stated that she did not want to make herself sick with drugs any more and only wished to try to enjoy each day as much as possible without the sickness and fatigue brought on by treatments that held little promise of a cure. Mark was in complete agreement, and I think somewhat relieved. I, however, was not happy in the least. I sat there and was steaming in my chair, as I felt let down and betrayed. It was like Mark and Denise had decided this between the two of them, and I was left out and not consulted with. I could not ... I would not ever give up! The tears began to roll out of my eyes, the anger filled my heart, and I told them both that I was in complete disagreement with this decision. I had been pro-grammed for fighting this monster, and I suppose if I had allowed myself to ever even dream of anything other than a complete victory then perhaps the fight would have been over a long time ago.

It took some time, but eventually I recognized the cour-age and wisdom it took for Denise to arrive at her decision. The cold truth was that there was nothing more that could be done. So Denise took it upon herself to let us know that she was not willing to even consider anything else. She simply wished to take the time she had left and enjoy every minute of it as much as was possible. Taking toxic chemicals *into* her body would only take *away* from that, and she knew it. The truth was that it took more courage and faith for Denise to call it quits than it did for me to want to continue the fight. I was the one who was being a coward.

With that in mind, we made plans for a trip to the mountains of North Carolina and had a wonderful time. We stayed at a Best Western there in Dillsboro, North Carolina right on a beautiful river where the ducks and rushing waters would wake us each morning. We road the Smoky Mountain Railroad, fished for rainbow trout, mined for gemstones, rafted the Nantahala River, inner tubed on Deep Creek, and pretty much had the time of our lives. Denise was struggling a little bit physically, as the tumors had begun to attack her spinal cord and weakened the strength of her legs, but she never complained and didn't skip a beat. She did everything the kids and I did and then some.

Naturally, she even witnessed to others she met on our travels and left people in awe. She changed the hearts of a father and young son on the train, talked to a young man about his drinking problem while tubing on Deep Creek, and consoled an elderly widow at a restaurant one night. The only sad thing that happened was the afternoon while we were inner tubing Richard mentioned that the four of us always paired up with he and mom and Raechel and I as partners. And he wondered out loud who was going to be his partner once mommy was gone It broke my heart.

We took a lot of pictures that summer; our favorite was one we took of Denise standing in a giant bed of vibrant yellow flowers. Later, we would use that photo to memorialize Denise; that is the picture I think most of us choose to remember of Denise. Her standing with outstretched arms in the midst of summer sun and springtime beauty as if to say, "Look at me. Look at my life. Look at all that God can do!"

After our trip to North Carolina, Denise's health really progressed downward quite rapidly. The tumors on her spine and two new tumors at the base of her brain made it difficult for her to handle the simplest of tasks because she had very little strength in her legs. Standing, walking, talking, and bathing all became major problems. Denise went to a walker and eventually into a wheelchair and hospice came into our home to help. We had to put a hospice bed downstairs in the living room because it was impossible for Denise to make her way up and down the stairs and she was bound to hurt herself trying to do so. The amazing thing was, however, that Denise never stopped living and never lived like she was dying. She spent time with the children and me; we went for walks (the children took turns pushing her wheelchair) and fished in the ponds as she looked on from her wheelchair.

I'll never forget on one occasion that Denise had a particularly difficult day. Denise suffered a violent seizure that morning while being watched by our friend Nancy Rider, the wife of our children's school administrator, Tom. I had to come home from work and give her some new medication to ease her symptoms, and although we warded off any more seizures, the seizure she suffered took a lot out of her. That night we were supposed to go to the school, as they were honoring the students who had achieved high grades and attendance ratings. Our daughter, Raechel, was on the Principles Honor Role and was one of the recipients honored that night. When the time came, I asked Denise if she wanted to still go to the school, and she emphatically said yes. I was shocked. That was all I needed to hear! Getting her there and home would be a challenge, but I figured if that was what she wanted to do then who was I to stop her. After some careful planning, off we went. Tom had heard from his wife what had happened to Denise that day, as it had really shaken Nancy up a bit and the stress from the ordeal had caused even her to stay home that evening and try to relax. Imagine his surprise when he saw Denise being wheeled down the center aisle at the start of the night's festivities. Denise's incredible spirit came through again and amazed us all once again. Denise was always very involved with our children's education, and she was so proud of Raechel's achievements she just loved being there that night.

On October 22, 2004, Denise and I celebrated our twelfth wedding anniversary. That afternoon my sister Dottie took care of Raechel and Richard, and I went home, picked up my wife, and took her to Fleming's Steak House to celebrate our big day. I had not planned the night and did not have a reservation, and the restaurant was booked solid. Looking back now, I feel bad that I hadn't planned a special night, but I was just becoming so overwhelmed by all that was happening, it was all I could do to keep up with the daily routine of working and taking care of the kids. When Dottie called me that afternoon, I simply realized that the opportunity had presented itself, so I'd be foolish not to make the most of it. The hostess told us we were welcome to dine on the patio if we liked. It was a beautiful fall evening, and we said yes and watched one of the most striking sunsets we had ever seen. I told Denise how much I loved her and thanked her for giving me the best twelve years of my life. I thanked her for being such a wonderful wife and told her what a terrific mother she had been to Raechel and Richard and what fine people they would be because of the time she had spent with them. She looked at me and smiled and said to me with a sparkle of love in her eyes, "Rod, thank you for making all of my dreams come true." Then she raised her glass of wine to mine and said, "Here is to heaven. I'll see you at the gates!" It was difficult for her to speak, as the tumors in her brain had really slowed her train of thought, but she managed to say more to me in those two sentences than most people could say in a lifetime.

A week later, the First Baptist Church where we attended was holding its annual Fall Festival. My sister, Dottie, and a few friends strolled Denise around the different gaming booths and asked her where she wanted to help out. Denise insisted on working the evangelism booth where the church witnessed to anyone who wanted to hear the message of Jesus Christ. Some time that night, seven young ladies stopped by, and Denise witnessed to them about her story and told them all that God had done for her. The seven of them professed their faith in Christ to Denise that night, and in unison, they gave their hearts over to the Lord. There was no stopping Denise, as she continued to impress and amaze all of us with her undying strength, faith, and spirit. She was truly God's champion.

Going Home

On the road marked with suffering
Though there's pain in the offering
Blessed be your name
Every blessing you pour out,
I turn back to praise
When the darkness closes in, Lord
Still I will say …
Blessed be the name of the Lord
Tree 63, "Blessed Be Your Name"[20]

As she slowly deteriorated, we had hospice come into our home to help us care for Denise. They provided all the necessary pain medications—free of charge and had their nurses scheduled for regular visits and on call twenty-four hours a day if we needed them. They provided us with other items we needed such as a wheelchair, walker, and specialty items that made showering and using the bathroom safer and easier for someone in Denise's condition. *What a wonderful organization.* I couldn't thank them enough and will always remember them when it is time to contribute to a worthy cause with either my time or my money.

Our desire was to keep Denise at home for as long as possible and then move her into the hospice house when it became absolutely necessary to do so. I wanted to have as much time with Denise as possible and allow her to spend time with our children while she still could. It may have been difficult for us to see her slipping away a little more each day, but I also think it allowed us to come to terms with it long before Denise actually died. Denise had daily visitors most of whom were friends she had made through my sister, Dottie, the Isle of Capri Christian Church, and the First Baptist Church of Naples. Denise remained very active in the Refresh-her bible study at First Baptist and many of these women volunteered to sit with Denise each afternoon while I was working in the restaurant. Dottie Scofield, Marion Bethea, Jody Vandeuser, Jackie Lee, Nancy Rider, Paula Bulmer, Janet Wicker, and Susan Blatz were her most frequent caregivers. They were incredibly helpful during a most difficult time, and I could never thank them enough. There were some who felt it was a mistake to keep Denise at home for as long as I did, but I honestly felt like I would just know instinctively when it was time to take her to hospice, and that was exactly what happened.

On Friday, November 5, 2004, it happened. I came down the stairs to get Denise up to take her to the bathroom, wash her, give her meds, and try to get some food into her stomach, and she was very unresponsive and generally uncooperative. I immediately called Hospice of Naples and asked them if they could get a room ready for Denise, and they said that they would have to see if they had a room available. I told them that I knew there was one available but would wait for them to call me back and confirm everything. I also told them I planned on bringing her down late that afternoon as long as it could be arranged. I know it sounds strange but I just knew, without a doubt that this is what was going to happen on that day. Dottie and Marion were with Denise that day, and I explained to them what was happening and that I would call them later with the details.

When I came home early that afternoon, I explained to Denise what was happening and that it was time to take her to Hospice. I think Denise understood what I was doing, but she really was having a difficult time putting any words together. I told Denise that I was unable to give her the care that she needed and deserved and that the nurses and doctors at hospice would be able to keep her much more comfortable and make sure that her medicines were given to her as needed. Naturally, they could give the meds by injection if necessary where as I could not. Denise was having trouble swallowing, and it was hard to give her food and water, let alone a barrage of pills every morning that could not be given on an empty stomach. Hospice admissions called me earlier in the day and told me what I already suspected, they had a room ready for Denise and I should bring her in and have her admitted sometime prior to four in the afternoon.

Once admitted I had to spend about an hour with the doctor assigned to Denise's case going over her medical history and what medications she is on and so on. It was actually kind of grueling. We were in Denise's room discussing it, and it felt awkward going over it all with Denise there but unable to partake in the discussion. She was very much alert and aware of what was happening but simply could not speak. It must have been very frustrating for her. Once we were through and Denise and I were finally alone, she leaned forward and rolled her finger to motion me toward her . I sat on her bed directly in front of her and inched close to her in anticipation of what she had to say. Her hand with the rolling finger was then made into a fist, and she said very clearly, "I'd like to punch you in the nose!"

I was somewhat taken aback because I felt like I had done everything I could to take the best care of Denise, and I wasn't really sure what I had done to upset my wife. She leaned back on her pillow and seemed satisfied that she had delivered her message to me as I asked her, "Denise, are you upset because I brought you here?" She nodded with a slow but deliberate yes. I was somewhat relieved because I knew I had done the right thing. I took a few minutes to tell Denise how much I loved her but that I was not capable of giving her the care she so desperately needed. I explained to her that I did not want her to suffer needlessly and only wanted her to have people around her continuously who could make her comfortable, feed her, bathe her, and deliver her meds to her as needed. I also told her that if her condition improved that we were free to leave any time we liked and I would bring her home. I think that is all she wanted to hear. She simply needed time to process what was happening, and she was not yet prepared for the end of her life to come, just yet.

I quickly got the word out to all our friends in Naples and Gainesville and our family members in Atlanta, New Smyrna, and Ft. Lauderdale that Denise was now at hospice and may only have days or perhaps weeks to live. Most people wanted to make a final visit and the first thing they wanted to know was when they should come. I didn't really know how to respond other than that they should come as soon as they could. I could not predict the timing of what was going to happen nor did I wish to. Over the next few days, people came to see Denise, and miraculously, Denise really seemed to perk up and enjoyed many visits from family and friends alike. For a day or so, I actually thought Denise was improving, but it was only temporary. People brought beautiful flowers, an angel whose wings would light up, and a miniature Christmas tree for Holiday Spirit. We brought in a CD player and kept Denise's favorite Christian tunes playing softly throughout each day.

I allowed a couple of local friends spend the night with her the first night or two and then decided to stay each night with her from then on until Denise had passed. Denise's best friend, Tammy Grosskopf, also came in that weekend and spent the last couple of nights of Denise's life, sleeping on a lounge chair next to Denise's bed. I slept on a cot on the screened porch so that Tammy could be close to Denise. I felt bad since I had taken Denise from Gainesville and all of the support she had there. The least I could do was allow Tammy to be next to Denise as much as possible.

It was really an incredible time, those last few days with Denise. People were there showing their love for Denise around the clock. They were reading scripture with her, singing hymns and her favorite Christian songs, massaging her hands and feet, stroking her hair and forehead, praying for and with her. It was extremely sad and painful but, at the same time, beautiful. At one point, as I was leaving the room with my buddy Dan , I turned to look at Denise as she was being doted over by several people at the same time. There were two people at her feet massaging her feet and legs, one on each side of the bed and a couple of others looking on. I said to Dan, "Wow, just look at that…what a way to go, huh? I don't think it's going to be like this when it is our time to go, do you?"

Dan smiled and looked troubled all at the same time and said, "Nope, my wife already told me she was just going to throw me in a ditch." We laughed and walked out of the room in amazement.

One of my friends from Cracklin' Jacks called me that evening to see how Denise or Neicy, as he liked to call her, was doing. I told him I didn't think she had much time left, and he said he was going to try and come for a visit the next day. Joe-Lee was one of my sales reps that I bought food and supplies from. He was keeping busy with work, and it had kept him from getting by for a visit. He said he would do his best to get by and decided to come by very early the next day, which ended up being five o'clock in the morning on November 10. He came in as we were all sleeping and came over to Denise's bedside, told her he loved her, and that it was okay if she wanted to go, that everyone would be just fine. He then said a sweet prayer and asked God to bring her home and stop her from suffering any longer.

He then walked out of the room, and the nurse came in to see how Denise was doing. A few minutes later I heard her say, "Denise just took her last breath." Tammy and I came to her side, and Tammy said her final goodbye and left the room. I leaned over Denise, put my head on her lap, and cried like a baby. My life with Denise was over, and it would be the saddest day of my life.

Dan spent a lot of time with us during our stay at hospice, and he wrote a beautiful piece that told of everything that happened there during those five final days, here it is.

Love is a Sweet Thing
A Day with Denise, Rod, and Friends
By: Dan Robinson
November 10, 2004

Yesterday Denise opened her eyes brightly for a
newborn babe
And Raechel, Little Richard, and Rod
The gentle touches, voices of family, friends,
teachers, and
Even a faint smile at the Hospice dog
Late that evening a mystical calmness settled over
the room
And somehow without words we all knew
All her close kin from Ft. Lauderdale, Atlanta and
far away
Had gathered there in the darkness
To sing her favorite hymn which somehow gave an
invitation
To bring her back to us one last time.
"Amazing Grace how sweet the sound
That saved a wretch like me
I once was lost
But now am found
Was blind but now I see"
All these lyrics rolled along like familiar surf
pounding

On the Naples sands not far away
But when everyone saw Denise's tears begin to flow
One drop at a time and roll down her soft swollen
cheeks
It felt as though I was the only one left singing off
key.
Through a room full of sniffles I reached down
deep for the words
As her hands lifted above her head in praise.
I was remembering all those who found amazing
grace though her
Broken body and the story of her life as we sang
"How precious did that grace appear the hour I first
believed?"
They asked me to read something from the Word, I
chose Isaiah 40
I then kissed her wet cheek, told her I loved her,
and that
God loved her as much as she loved Him
She somehow lifted her head, opened wide her
doe-like eyes
Grabbed my hand and said, "Don't leave me."
I sat beside her, held her and wept.
I later told her goodbye as I felt her spirit would
soon be leaving
This body that had given so much to others.
Within a few hours just before daybreak at 5:40 Joe
Lee eased in
With Rod and Tammy nearby, Joe Lee wanted to
pray with her
He came by to tell God that she had suffered long
enough

He whispered to God to please take her on home
and it was okay
He told Denise that he loved her and he would
never forget her
Joe Lee put his hand on her and walked out of the
room.
Moments later Denise belonged to the ages
A Hospice lady came down the hall to tell me and
as I
Moved into her room the moon was coming up
under Venus
Which aligned with a star and it was a beautiful
morning
As I gazed across her patio and the water as Rod
stood staring
I knew what he had lost because "Love is a Sweet
Thing"
Yet Denise's Spirit lives within Rod and the
children
Her Spirit moves around Cracklin' Jacks
It moves around Bonita Springs and Naples
It moves around Naples and Ft. Lauderdale
It moves around Atlanta, California, NIH, Shands
and the South
It moves around in the hearts of so many like
Camille and mine
At the churches she loved so much for long like
Trinity United Methodist Church
For it was through her love and her faith despite
her illness
That so many came to know the God we all love.
Rod wants all to have the faith that she had
He is no different than Jesus in that regard

It is a passion that all should come to know the love
of God
Denise was a model of faith to the end as it never
wavered
We had dinner with her in Gainesville after her last
treatment
Just a few days ago and she told me how much God
loved me
With only a few days left, on October 29, Rod's
sister, Dottie
Shared with us a story that is part of Denise's
Legacy
The families were going to the Fall Festival and
Dottie asked her
If she wanted to work at one of the playful booths
Denise said, "Oh no, I want to work the
Evangelism Booth"
From her wheelchair that night seven new souls
invited
The love of God into their hearts and gave their life
to Christ
In one night during her last days she did this, and
wondered
How many came to a closer walk with God during
her
All too short a life with us
And then I asked myself the tough question,
Have I invited seven lately to know how sweet love
is?
I looked across the room and their Gainesville
hostess, Tammy,
Who was gently massaging her dear friend's feet

She was touching the anklet that had been her gift
of love
Rod would later return it when Tammy and I
sat with Rod as he made plans at Fullers Funeral
Home
Rod's older brother and childhood fishing buddy,
Richard
Reached over with wife, Sandy, in hand
They gently hung over Denise and whispered
goodbye
As they hugged her I witnessed something few do
I actually saw Denise's love move out of her body
And into them
Rod must have seen it too as he handed his
Most sacred thing in the world to Richard and said
Denise tabbed all these books in here for me and all
my favorite scriptures are underlined
I gave Richard and Sandy a hug I felt their love
Richard turned and said, "Dan" and I said "Yes?"
"Was that Isaiah 40?"
I said "Yes"
I'm going to read it.
I said, "Maybe Sandy can read it to you as you drive
back to
Ft. Lauderdale."
I told Rod he had a wonderful family as I saw the
love between him
and Debbie, Donna, Dottie and Richard and their
spouses like Sandy and Dane.
I know when all our cloudy days come we will
remember that day
And even with the dozens of tumors that ravaged
her body

The Light never went our of her Eyes
The Fight never went of her Body
The Spirit never went out of her Witness
The Truth never went out of her Soul
And her Sweet Love never went out of her Heart.

But what I choose to remember most about Denise
was her humor
The Trickster Energy never went out of her Angel
Her long time friend Sandy Miller was holding her
hand:

When I rolled into town
Sandy stayed by her side all day and into the
evening
She set her alarm clock for 7 a.m. this morning
But rather the clock awoke her at 5:45 a.m. right on
time
I just bet that Denise had a little smile on her face
As she flew by under her own power
I can feel the touch of angels' wings as I sit at
Denise and Rod's
Dining room table and scribble this out
Can you feel them now?
It is her Trickster Energy that reminds us all that
the lyrics
Of Faith Hill's beautiful song about reaching out to
those different from us which is what Denise's life
was all about:
Love is a Sweet Thing

The Enemies Within

Enemy
One that is antagonistic to another; especially one
seeking to injure, overthrow, or confound an opponent.
Something harmful or deadly.
A military adversary, a hostile unit or force.
Merriam-Webster Dictionary[21]

As I said earlier, I read a book called *There's Hope* by Richard
Bloch who had been diagnosed with lung cancer and wanted
to reach out to help others stricken with cancer. One of the
things that stood out for me was where he talked about finding your support team in helping with this fight you have been
assigned to. He talked about not only finding the right doctors
who are knowledgeable and skilled in their works but also in
which family members and friends would have an active role
with your private war on cancer. What he said made perfect
sense to me, but what I did not realize was how it would feel
to have to deal with the ones who were not capable, for one
reason or another, of helping us in our situation.

The other part of this that I was not ever ready for was
in dealing with the people who *were* capable but were simply not willing to do what was right and just. These are the

people that really turn my stomach inside out and are the hardest to forgive; fortunately, there are only a few. I think that is a big reason for this chapter, for forgiveness.

The enemies I refer to in this chapter are not people who truly wish to do any harm to Denise or me. There is no malice or seeking to injure or any hostility really. They are simply people who failed to help us in any measurable way, and in some cases, they may have actually done harm and perhaps even contributed to Denise's death. I may never know for certain. However, just the same, when someone or something plays a part in taking away what is most treasured and dear, some ugly feelings surface.

I believe that dealing with these feelings and all my feelings at this time is the driving force behind this book. It is therapy for me. Writing has always been a good way for me to unload the feelings that are stuffed into the deepest crevices of my soul, and this chapter is going to go there. In fact, this chapter will reach not only the deepest crevices, but the darkest and scariest ones too.

The wonderful thing about Jesus is that he has a way of shining a light on these places in your life if you reveal them and ask for his help, and once he does then you will be able to heal and to grow and this is what I'm after. I pray that he will recognize this and help me to wash this area of my heart clean once and for all. I wish to heal and learn from my experiences. Then I will be able to move on and use what I've learned to help someone else. That gives a great purpose to my life and my sufferings. What more could I ask for?

At the time of Denise's diagnoses, Denise was busy rearing two very small children. Raechel was a two-year-old and Richard was just three months old. Naturally, we were quite shocked with the news that was delivered to us and so were our friends. Denise had been involved with a playgroup at the time. Karen Twist and Cindy Spiegel were part of this playgroup, Denise had begun to get to know them, and we occasionally did some things with them on a social level. On one rare occasion, we took our pontoon boat over to the Rainbow River with Karen, her husband, Jim, and their daughter, April. Of course, we brought our two little ones, Raechel and Richard, also. We were not real close friends, but perhaps we could have been.

Karen pulled away from Denise after she was given her terrible news. She was stunned and uncomfortable with it, and she was simply unable to be of any help to Denise at what was a very stressful and sad time in Denise's life. Denise felt abandoned and let down, although over time I think she began to understand what had happened.

I recognized it immediately; it was very much the same as what had happened with Dr. Jackson. The biggest difference was that we were not really friends with Dr. Jackson, she was just our doctor, and the Twist's were our friends. Cindy was very close to Karen, and I think Cindy just kind of fell into the same hole that Karen did. I told Denise that these people did not mean to harm her or hurt her feelings. It was just that they had probably never had to deal with anything like this before, and they simply did not know what to do. In addition, they were in a magical time of their lives, raising young children, and rejoicing in that. Dealing with someone else's cancer was simply not something they wished to deal with.

I encouraged Denise to simply let it go, to know that these were not the people we needed to have as part of our support group. Actually, it was good to know where we stood with them. I also encouraged Denise to try and forgive them. I explained to her that they had no idea how the way they dealt with this situation hurt her and they had no intentions of doing so. It just happened. I know that this was very difficult for Denise. However, I also know that the closer Denise became with the Lord, the more she was able to forgive others, and surely, she could forgive Karen and Cindy.

Interestingly, during the week of Denise's memorial service, I ran into Cindy in the local coffee shop where Denise used to frequently meet with friends. As I sat and visited with some friends, I recognized Cindy as she came in for some coffee. I was hoping she wouldn't see or recognize me, as I was afraid she had not heard of Denise's death. I was really struggling at the time and just didn't want to explain it to another person, especially not someone who had abandoned Denise the way Cindy had. As luck would have it, she sat down at the table next to me and immediately caught my eye.

She said hello and asked the customary, "How is Denise?"

I walked over to her table to give her the news. "I'm sorry to tell you that Denise has passed away," I said calmly. I didn't give her much opportunity to respond; I simply told her that the kids and I were doing fine and that it was good that Denise was no longer suffering and had gone home to be with Jesus. I walked away and could only imagine how she must have felt.

When Denise was diagnosed with a recurrence of new cancer to the lymph nodes in her neck, we had decided to try radiation as a means to prevent future problems. Cindy's dad was a local radiologist, and we decided to consult with him over the phone to see what he would recommend. What he proposed was a four to five week course of low dose radiation. The problem was that I had done much research and was aware that low dose radiation had been proven absolutely ineffective against melanoma. When I discussed this with him, he just said that this is what is recommended, and he thought we should proceed right away.

I asked him how many melanoma patients he had treated and he told me, "Just one." I should have asked him if the patient was still alive, but I think I already knew the answer and didn't wish to embarrass him. I told him that I would be in touch once we had made our decision. I consulted with another radiologist from Shands Hospital, and we discovered a new way of delivering high-dose radiation that had been proven safe and effective. We decided to use this treatment, and Denise never recurred to this area of her neck again. This is just one example of how a doctor can give terrible advice about a disease he knows absolutely nothing about.

There is no question that I was more knowledgeable and informed about the disease we were fighting. After I had learned about this new way of delivering the high-dose radiation, I even called him and asked him if he could perform this newer, more advanced type of treatment. I was afraid my insurance would not allow me to use the people at Shands since Dr. Spiegel was who I was referred to. Even then, he still wanted to use the low dose procedure, as he was not familiar with this newer form of treatment. *How could that be? Was it arrogance, ignorance, or simply a case of mal-practice?* I believe that he simply was not aware of how to perform the newer treatment and was uncomfortable with doing so. *Understandable, so why not refer the patient to someone more qualified? Perhaps it is simple economics, and the doctor simply did not want to lose the business. The problem is that once you choose a treatment and perform it there is no turning back.* If we had gone with his recommendation, it is possible that the disease would have spread much sooner and much faster than it did and years of life could have been stolen from Denise, her children, and me. Thankfully, I was cautious enough to make the right choice. And I learned then and there that nobody could be trusted, nobody.

Ironically, the people who did Denise and me the biggest injustice of all were the same folks who probably added as many years to Denise's life as anyone. The John Wayne Cancer Institute had developed a melanoma vaccine that seemed to keep Denise's cancer at bay for many years. For the first two to three years, the only problem that arose was with a recurrence of cancer in the lymph nodes on Denise's neck. This could have been old cancer, left behind from surgery a year prior to the recurrence. The surgery was performed a second time to remove these new affected lymph nodes, and the cancer was gone. There was never a metastasis to any other area of the body while the vaccine was in use. For this to happen to a melanoma patient with stage III disease as aggressive as Denise's is quite remarkable.

As I recall, it was on a December trip when I received a phone call from Denise, and she was extremely upset. I was at the church helping to plan a men's ministry called "Petra" when I got the very disturbing call.

"Rod, I'm here at John Wayne, and they are refusing to give me the vaccine!" she exclaimed.

"What in the world are you talking about?" I asked.

"They said that I have had too many recurrences; therefore, I have to come off of the vaccine."

"You mean to tell me that they had you fly three thousand miles just to tell you that they weren't going to treat you any more?" I asked, as the blood started to boil inside of me. Denise went on to tell me that they said the way the protocol is written, a patient must be taken off the trial once they have had three or more recurrences. Naturally, this made no sense to me since the doctor had explained that the vaccine probably did not treat the brain in the first place. "Put Dr. Emmerson on the phone right now!" I screamed.

It was all I could do to not reach through the phone lines and put my hands around his throat. He tried to explain to me why Denise had to come off the treatment.

I said, "First of all, Dr. Emmerson, you don't have a patient fly three thousand miles and go through all the ordeal and expense to do that only to tell them they are no longer being treated; that is number one! Secondly, if you don't give her the vaccine that she came there for then I am catching the next jet to L.A., and you and I will have to discuss this in person. And the best thing we have going for us at this moment is that I am three thousand miles away. The last thing you would want right now would be for me to be sitting there with you in your office! Do you understand? Thirdly, after Denise receives her treatment today, you and I will need to sit down and discuss what is happening either over the phone or in your office, but right now I am so upset that we will have to wait until I've had some time to calm down."

I paused to catch my breath and give Emmerson a chance to respond. "Okay," he said, "Denise will be given the vaccine and then you can give me a call when you are ready, and we will discuss what is happening," he said quietly.

"So she is going to be treated today then?"

"Yes she will," he replied.

"Alright then, please put Denise back on the phone." I spoke with Denise, and we calmed each other down, as we had done so many times before. I told her everything would be fine, and she would get her vaccine. I would work things out with Emmerson after she came home. We were both in a total state of shock and could not believe the hospital that had done so much for us was trying to pull the rug out from under us without as much as a courtesy phone call. This was by far the most incredible, unbelievable circumstance I had been faced with since our ordeal began. I walked away from that phone call thinking, *How in the world could they be doing this to us after we had come this far?*

A few days after Denise had returned I set up a conference phone call with Dr. Emmerson and his protocol nurse, Kathy. He tried in vain to explain to me how the protocol would be put at risk if they kept patients on the trial after they had failed the vaccine. He said the FDA was very strict, and their trial could be shut down if they did not follow the protocol to the letter. I reminded him that her metastasis was all contained in her brain where he had told me the vaccine did not reach. He changed his tune on that and claimed that they were not sure if the vaccine treated the brain or not; there was no research to prove it one way or the other. I argued then that it was possible that the vaccine did not treat the brain, in which case it would not matter how many brain tumors there were. The vaccine was working and keeping her body cancer free.

I told him that we were being successful treating the brain lesions with radiation. In addition we had just begun a new trial experimenting with a combination of Temodar and Thalidomide. This only gave him more ammunition as he claimed that using these drugs compromised their study and could even work against the vaccine thus causing it to be impotent. That is when I decided to tell them how I really felt, and this time there would be no holding back.

"Dr Emmerson, let me summarize what has happened and tell you what I really think is happening here. First of all, you have Denise fly all the way out there only to tell her that she is being taken off the vaccine and won't be treated that day. Do you have any idea the amount of stress you caused her and how that has an impact on her health? You go on and on about your protocol and your rules and regulations and not once have you mentioned what is best for the patient, who happens to be my wife! In addition, you argue that the brain tumors are considered recurrences, even though you told me that you do not believe the vaccine treats the brain. If that is true, then there would be no logical reason to take her off the vaccine. This would only open her up to further metastasis in her body, which would be suicidal. Now then, I am not the sharpest tool in the shed, but I do consider myself full of common sense, and I must have some logical explanations in order for me to accept what you are doing to my wife. Here is what I believe to be the truth, such as it is. I believe that you all know that Denise is probably going to die from a brain tumor, sooner or later, probably sooner. And, you are conducting a clinical trial so that you can receive FDA approval and sell your product on the open market. I'm sure there are millions of dollars at stake here. However, in order for you to get the approval from the FDA, you must be able to show promising results from your clinical trial. Therefore, it is detrimental to your program to have patients dying from brain tumors while they are on your protocol, and that is exactly why you wish to take Denise off the trial before she dies!"

Kathy was quite beside herself at what I had said, but Emmerson didn't have much to say. I think I was right and he knew it. I went on to tell him, "The one thing you don't want to do when a patient is struggling is to rock the boat. Even if the vaccine is failing, which it is not taking her off the treatment would have emotional and mental ramifications that could cause Denise to lose her will to keep fighting ."

Then I asked him *the* question as I knew Emmerson was a family man with a newborn son at home. "If this was your wife and all the circumstances were the same, would you take your wife off of this vaccine?"

There was quite a long pause before he responded, "Yes."

"You sir, are a liar," I said without hesitation. "I'm sorry, but you took too long to give your answer," I finished. Sadly,

I knew I was right, and so did he. Then I asked him if I could speak to whoever would be the next up on the totem pole, and he gave me the name of a Dr. Shay.

I contacted Dr. Shay and had a very similar conversation with him until we were both exasperated. Later, I wrote a three-page letter and sent it to both Dr. Emmerson and Dr. Shay along with a testimonial to Christ that I had written. The testimonial included all the wonderful things God had done to keep Denise alive along with providing the vaccine for us. I was very much amazed when Dr. Emmerson called one day to say that they had decided to allow Denise to remain on the vaccine. I considered this a truly amazing and surprising victory for our side. However, Denise soon recurred in the brain once again several months later, and this time she was removed from the program for good. Dr. Emmerson assured me that because she had been vaccinated for such a long time that the vaccine would remain in her system for a good thirty months or so. I felt they never provided us with any other options or ever talked about what was best for Denise. It was always about their study and what was good for the trial, the FDA, and their rules and regulations and such; it is still very difficult for me to understand how they could be so callous.

Dr. Emmerson was right about one thing though. Almost thirty months later to the day, Denise was found to have a metastasis to her liver, a death sentence for a patient with melanoma. Eighteen months later, after numerous liver treatments and high dose IL-2 treatments performed with two weeks in ICU Denise finally succumbed to a couple of large tumors at the base of her brain. Her disease had spread all over her body from head to toe, and her final days were miserable.

The only saving grace was that it was a brain tumor that took her life and not the liver disease. Denise had survived over thirty-two brain tumors over a five-year period, something the folks at John Wayne had never thought possible. We'll never know what could have been had Denise been allowed to stay on the vaccine. At the very least, perhaps we would not have had to deal with all the disease in her body that caused her so much unnecessary pain and discomfort. Or, maybe the vaccine would have suppressed the brain disease, and Denise would still be alive today being a wife to me and a mother to her two darling children. Unfortunately, it will remain a mystery to me. What I do know is that the John Wayne Cancer Institute did a terrible disservice to Denise, a patient of theirs who was at their mercy and was treated like a number. Even though they probably added more years to her life than anyone else did, they were very wrong for how they performed, and that is why they are now considered an enemy in my book.

After Denise had recurred a couple of times with brain metastasis, I became very active in trying to come up with a chemical solution to her brain disease. The Radiosurgery worked very well, but I was told that there was going to be a point in time where we would not be able to keep treating her with radiation. They really weren't sure how many lesions could be treated, but it certainly was not an indefinite amount, and that scared the life out of me.

My research took us to Ft. Lauderdale for a brain tumor conference held by The Brain Tumor Society. We met with a wonderful doctor named Debra Heros. She introduced us to a new technique using two very old drugs in conjunction with each other.

Dr. Heros gave me all the information to give to our oncologist, and I thought, *Great, we'll get Denise started on this right away. Enough experimentation had been done to show the safe and effective doses to use so there would be no harm in giving it a try.* Much to my amazement and disappointment, things were not that simple.

We took our findings to our next scheduled visit with Dr. Rob Martin, Denise's oncologist, a pleasant man from South Africa who was always kind and attentive to Denise and seemed fairly knowledgeable. Once I presented him with all the information, he said he would look into it and get back to me as soon as he could. Several days went by and I grew impatient. All I could think of is how this therapy was immediately available, not harmful but not being used. So, I sent Dr. Martin an e-mail asking him if he had looked at the therapy yet and that we were anxious to get the ball rolling. He e-mailed me back and said he had been very busy and would get to it as soon as he could.

Several more days passed and my impatience was turning into frustration and anger. I typed him another e-mail, and although I was polite, I did mention that I felt we were wasting valuable time that we could ill-afford to lose. That really upset him, which is the last thing I needed to have happen. He e-mailed me back, told me that he had many patients of which we were only one and he was doing the best he could do. When I tried to respond to let him know that wasn't good enough, my e-mail came back "return to sender" as he had put a block on my e-mail address, thus cutting off our line of communication and letting me know that he did not wish to hear from me again. Not only did I find this response inappropriate and unacceptable but cowardly as well.

I decided to vent my frustration with another doctor, our radiologist and friend, Dr. Bill Mendenhall. He told me that he had heard of problems like this in the past with Dr. Martin. Mostly that he was overworked and understaffed and was very, very slow dealing with patients like us. He decided that it might be a good idea for us to schedule an appointment with a different oncologist rather than trying to get Dr. Martin to help. So he put us in touch with Dr. Chong, someone he thought was very good and would be willing to go the extra mile for us. This turned out to be another very frustrating experience.

Of course, we had to wait another two to three weeks just to get in to see the man. Then when we got in front of him, not only was he not interested in this new therapy we had discovered, he did not want to speak with me at all. He directed all of his questions and attention to Denise because after all, she is the patient and this is her life we were talking about. The problem was Denise did not want to have to deal with all of these types of decisions. The research and treatment options were always left up to me. And this really worked well for us because trying to make life and death decisions tend to be quite stressful, and stress presents an unnecessary burden on ones immune system. Therefore, Denise and I worked as a team, I find the treatments, and she tolerates them. Dr. Chong didn't seem to understand our way of doing things. He kept asking her technical questions about her former treatments and such, which she had difficulty answering correctly. So, I kept butting in and giving him the correct answers and this seemed to annoy him.

Finally, he began to engage me and asked if I had considered taking Denise to the Moffitt Center in Tampa, Florida a couple of hours from Gainesville. I felt like saying, "Oh we wouldn't dream of it; we thought it would be much easier to go to Maryland, California, and Miami before giving them a try." Of course, I had spoken to several doctors at the Moffitt Center and knew quite well that there was nothing there for us, and I told Dr. Chong as much.

Naturally, he didn't think I knew what I was talking about. He asked if I had met with a specific doctor there, I forget his name now, but I told him no. Ironically, while at the Brain Tumor Conference I had spoken with a Dr. Steven Brem who was the chief neurologist with the Moffitt Center. Dr. Brem assured me that there was nothing available for us there. I told Dr. Chong that I had spoken with several doctors at the Moffitt Center, including a personal chat with Steve Brem and several phone conversations with the oncologist there handling all the clinical trials on melanoma.

This wasn't good enough for Dr. Chong, so he decided it would be best if he called a doctor there that he knew to see what "they" could do for us. I invited him to do so and hoped he would get an answer from them before we finished our visit with him. He left the room, made the call, came back, and, allowed me to explain this new therapy to him. In the mean time, a doctor from Moffitt returned his call, and he left the room. *This should be interesting*, I thought to myself.

Twenty minutes later, he returned with a very somber look on his face. He sat in front of us and looking quite depressed, explained to us that the Moffitt center had nothing available to us, and there was nothing that they could do. It took all the strength and patience in my soul to not say something I would surely regret. I could not afford to burn another bridge. Instead, I said. "Dr. Chong, please don't sit there looking all sad like your telling us something we don't already know. I have spoken with doctors all around the country and understand exactly what we are dealing with, and so does Denise! Now then, we have uncovered a new therapy that has shown some promise against brain mets from melanoma and were hoping that you would help us to give it a try."

The man sat there for the next thirty minutes trying to explain to me why we should not go on this new therapy. He told me that it was unproven and even if it did work against Denise's disease that we would never know if it actually was the cure or not because we were not using it in a clinical trial setting. He went on to tell me that what we would learn would not help anybody else since we would not be in a formal clinical trial.

I asked him if he thought the therapy would be harmful to Denise, and he said he did not think so. The doses were very low, the drugs were quite old, and their effects were well known. He only thought it could be harmful if use was permitted for a number of years. I only hoped we had a number of years left in Denise's life with which to use it. I had to make one last-ditch effort to get him to help us and I said, "Dr. Chong, I know that my wife is probably going to die from a brain tumor. I also know that there is nothing 100% proven that we can try to prevent that from happening. However, these doctors in Miami are using this therapy and have seen some effectiveness of it against brain metastasis from melanoma. Please help us by administering it to Denise and monitoring her progress, we really need your help here."

Dr. Chong left the room and returned to say that he could not be of any help to us. He asked me if I had ever spoken with Dr. Kirkwood with the University of Pittsburgh. I told him that I had heard of him and read about him, but I had not actually ever spoken to him directly. He gave me his number and asked me to give him a call. I told him that I would, and I would let him know what he had to say. Later that same day I called and asked for Dr. Kirkwood, and the nurse explained to me that the doctor never speaks to patients or spouses directly, that he would only speak to our doctor, I wanted to scream. I called Dr. Chong's office back and explained that Dr. Chong would have to call Dr. Kirkwood himself and let me know what he had to offer. I never hear from Dr. Chong again, even after placing several more calls to his office. *Unbelievable!*

Out of desperation, I told Denise that if she wanted to be treated locally with this new therapy she would have to somehow mend fences with Dr. Martin. I asked her to e-mail him from her e-mail account and apologize if I had done anything to upset him. She did so and told him that this was childish and unfair to her and she needed his help.

He responded and also apologized and agreed that we all needed to work together for what was best for Denise.

We met once again, and he asked me what we would like to do. I told him we wanted for Denise to be put in the combination therapy as soon as possible.

I could not believe it when he asked, "Are you sure this is what you want to do?"

Calmly I said, "Yes, it is." He then proceeded to write the prescription. Denise went nearly one entire year without any further brain metastasis, and it was such a wonderful thing. Her neurologist, Dr. Bill Friedman, was pleasantly surprised, and after on follow up MRI almost a year later, asked us what we were doing to have had such success for such a long time. We told him "prayer and this new treatment," and he told us that whatever it was to keep on doing it. About that same time, Dr. Martin told us that the therapy was now in the medical journal as having been proven effective against brain metastasis from melanoma and other cancers. We were not surprised. Unfortunately, our enemies were not through with us yet!

Dr. Martin discovered through routine blood tests that Denise's liver enzymes were highly elevated. As a precaution, he decided to stop the therapy of Thalidomide and Temodar and see if this was the cause for the elevated levels. After two weeks or so, if this were the cause, the levels should return to normal. Two weeks went by and nothing had changed. Two more weeks and again the levels were still high. I asked Dr. Martin to put her back on the therapy, and he said he was uncomfortable with doing so. I asked him what were we going to do, and he seemed confused and unsure.

I said, "We need to get this resolved, so Denise can get back on her cancer treatment. Do you want us to see a liver specialist or what?" He suggested we talk to her primary physician, Dr. Hal Brooks and ask him for his advice. I thought this seemed like a step down but figured maybe he knew what he was doing. I thought, *Besides, what choice do I have?*

We met with Dr. Brooks and explained the situation to him. The only other drugs Denise was taking at the time were her thyroid medicine, Synthroid, and an anti-seizure drug called Dylantin. The Dylantin had been in use for a number of years so nobody suspected this as the cause. Denise was taken off of the Synthroid and again her blood tests remained the same with elevated liver enzymes. Brooks decided to go another two weeks and repeat the labs at that time. I always had the results faxed to our home, so I could review them and compare them to past results. I trusted no-one. I was becoming increasingly frustrated with this nonchalant attitude. Nobody seemed to care that Denise had been taken off her cancer therapy and could be left exposed for more brain tumors. After all, she had gone nearly a year now without a recurrence. This was by far the longest stretch of time without any more cancer. *Did they think it was only a coincidence? What if the reprieve was due solely to the effects of the Temodar/Thalidomide regimen?* She had now been off the therapy for over two months, and there was absolutely no sense of urgency among any of the doctors who were treating Denise. *Am I the only one who cares?* Sadly, I was.

Two more weeks went by and Denise went for her results without me this time. When I came home, I found the test results on the fax and nothing had changed. The liver enzymes were still elevated. The only thing that made sense to me would be to take Denise off the Dylantin and see what happened. My neighbor across the street and I had been discussing it; he was a pharmacist. I had also been researching Dylantin on the Internet and had learned that it was a drug that was absorbed by and could be toxic and harmful to the liver. Surely, Dr. Martin and Dr. Brooks were privy to this information! I also had been speaking to a close friend, Dan Robinson, about the situation. Dan was a professor of pharmacy at the University of Florida, and he and I often spoke about Denise's care. He would also help me to research different approaches and keep an eye out for any new treatments that looked promising. Dan and I talked about a chemical in Dylantin called Phenetoin that was very toxic to the liver. I began to understand that this just had to be the culprit; it was the only logical explanation.

When Denise came home, I asked her about her visit with Dr. Brooks. She said everything was fine, and he told her that her results looked a little improved!

"What are you talking about? What is improved?" I asked.

"I don't know what exactly he meant, Rod, he just said that things looked better." I looked at the results again and was dumb-founded. There must be something there that the untrained eye just cannot see. I had actually done research on the Internet on all of the blood tests listed on the lab reports.

I tried to educate myself so that I would have a good under-standing of what all the different results meant, but I knew that I was still just a restaurant manager. The doctors should know a lot more than I did. Or so I'd hoped.

"What else did Brooks have to say?" I probed further. I was upset at myself for missing that appointment. Denise never knew how to ask the right questions of the doctors and then had a hard time remembering what it was they told her in the first place. "He said my Dylantin levels were too low, so he increased my prescription." I couldn't believe my ears.

"Why in the world did he do that?" I asked.

"I don't know, Rod. He said the level was low on my blood tests, so it should be increased. Stop asking me so many questions. If you want to know more then just call him up." She said. It was still before five o'clock on a Monday, and I thought I'd better give him a call and ask him to explain it to me. Not only did it not make sense that the results were improved, but he increased the one drug that I suspected was giving her the trouble with her liver; this was another night-mare in the making. I called his office and left a message for him to call me as soon as possible.

The next day I decided to call Dr. Friedman, Denise's neurologist and ask him his opinion on the Dylantin. I also told Denise not to fill the prescription for the higher dose until I told her to do so. Dr. Friedman was the one who pre-scribed the drug in the first place because it was being used as a precaution against possible seizures. If a tumor appeared in just the wrong place Denise would be prone to a seizure, and this could prevent that from happening. I left a message with his assistant, Lorraine, and he called me back a few hours later. That was one of the things I loved about Bill; he was always available to me. He had great compassion for what I was going through and respected me for the efforts I made; he and I had become friends.

"Hello Rod, what's going on?" he asked.

"Oh, hi, Bill. Thanks for returning my call. I'm concerned because Denise's primary physician increased the level of Dylantin on her prescription, and I thought you should know about it. Is there any reason why he should have done this?" I asked.

"What are her symptoms? Has Denise had a seizure, or is she having any headaches or some other problems I need to know about?" he quizzed.

"No, sir, nothing at all, that's why I'm calling. He said that her blood test showed a low level of the drug, and that is why he is doubling the dose from 100mg to 200mg." I responded.

"Rod, if she hasn't had a seizure, a headache, or any symptoms whatsoever then there is absolutely no reason to increase the dose. Do not fill the prescription and call me if you have any problems," he stated matter-of-factly as he usually did.

"Okay, thanks again, Bill. I appreciate your time, and I'll take care of it." I said as I hung up the phone.

Another day went by, and Brooks still had not returned my call. On Wednesday, I put in another call and left my second message. By Friday, I had still not heard back from Dr. Brooks, and now I was extremely upset. The weekend was here, and I was headed out of town to take the family to SeaWorld for the weekend. On our way, there I decided to call Brooks's office for the fourth time. I had called and left my message that morning, and by four o'clock there was still nothing.

I called again, and the nurse on the phone told me that Dr. Brooks was gone for the weekend. My blood began to boil. "I have been calling all week. Did he not receive any of my messages?" I fumed.

"Yes sir. Mr. Ellis, he did receive your messages. I don't know why he did not return your calls," she said.

"I am extremely upset, and I really need to talk to him. What will it take for me to do that?" I asked.

"Would you like to make an appointment?" she asked politely.

"If that's what it takes then absolutely. Can you get me in on Monday?" I asked.

"Yes, Monday afternoon for his last appointment might be best since you seem to have a lot to talk about, and he will have more time for you then. How does four o'clock sound to you?" she asked.

"Four o'clock on Monday is perfect. I'll see you then." I finished the call and hung up the phone.

Denise and I came together for the appointment and waited for Brooks to come out. He came to the waiting room, and we held our meeting there since there was nobody else around. I could tell he was agitated and defensive. I'm sure he knew how upset I was because I had not held back my feelings with his staff.

"What seems to be the problem?" he asked abruptly.

"Well, first of all I'd like to know why after leaving several phone messages with you I never heard back from you." I was not going to be intimidated by this quack.

"I don't see why I need to explain test results to your wife and then waste my time explaining it to you a second time. I am very busy here, and when you called, I was on my way to take my son to boy-scouts," he said bluntly.

"Well, I'm very sorry to interfere with your family time, but when I call to speak to you, that is because I have questions about my wife's situation, and I have to talk to you. By the way, I called three or four times, and you neglected to return a single call. Now then, if I have to make an appointment to talk to you, I'm happy to do so. Or, if you prefer, I could use e-mail since you don't like to use the phone. Whatever is most convenient for you is fine with me, but when I have questions, we have to talk." I was firm and angry. I think he was beginning to realize that we were alone in the room together, and my eyes were scaring him just a bit as I began to give him the "Ellis stare." He softened his stance and apologized for not having called me back. He said he would give me his e-mail address, and I could feel free to e-mail him any time I had a concern.

"What else can I help you with?" he asked. "Denise said that you told her the liver results looked improved. Can you explain that to me?" I asked as I put the results in front of him.

"Well, some of the numbers are slightly improved although they are still very much on the high side of the range. I think we should repeat the tests again in another week and see what they have to say at that time," he responded.

"I also want to know why you increased her level of Dylantin," I stated.

"Simple," he smirked. "The blood tests show that the level is so low that it would be considered ineffective. Naturally, the level should be brought up into the normal range." He looked at me as if I was an idiot and should not be trying to play doctor. I'd seen that look many times before.

"Interesting," I said. "However, you are not the one who prescribed the Dylantin in the first place. That job belongs to Dr. Friedman, Denise's neurologist, and if the level is going to be changed, it should come from him. And, as a matter of fact, I called Bill last week, and he said there is absolutely no reason for the Dylantin to be increased whatsoever. We decided to leave the prescription as it were. Don't you think it would make sense to consult with her neurologist, since he is the one in charge of treating Denise's brain?" *Oh, that felt good to say.*

"I cannot talk to Dr. Friedman," he responded as Denise, and I looked on with amazement. "Listen, Dr. Brooks, Denise has many doctors that we have put together as a team. Don't you think it makes sense that we all work together to make sure that Denise gets the best care possible?" I asked.

"Dr. Friedman and I had some problems when we were in medical school, and I cannot talk to him. That's all there is to it."

Denise and I were both in a total state of disbelief at what he had just said. I knew that we had just reached a new level of mediocrity and absurdity, and there was no point of going any further with this conversation. I wanted to choke him on the spot, but I was afraid that I would need a copy of Denise's records and didn't want any trouble when we took our business elsewhere as I knew we were going to have to do. I told him that that was all I needed to hear, and we would be on our way.

As we left his office, I looked at Denise and said, "He's

fired; you won't be seeing him again." It was kind of a shame because Denise always said she liked him and felt comfortable with him as a primary physician. But she fully understood what had just happened, and there was no need for us to discuss it. We had now wasted three months of time without Denise being on her therapy, and it looked like we were getting nowhere. It was time for a new approach. I knew it. Denise knew it.

I called my friend Dan Robinson and explained the situation, and he also could not believe what happened. He had spoken highly of his own family doctor, whom I had actually met at our men's group once or twice. I asked for his e-mail address, so I could ask for his help. I was tired of wasting time with these doctors, and I wanted to put everything in a letter to any new doctor we may hire. I was going to approach it as if I was interviewing them for the job, and there would be no misunderstanding that they, if they accepted my conditions, would be working for me. I decided at least this way I would not have to worry about all the niceties and politics of the relationship. This was going to be all business, and everything would be laid out on the table from the very beginning, all of our history, all of what we were trying to accomplish, and most importantly all of my expectations.

I wrote the letter and saved it to my computer in case I needed it in the future. The letter went into great detail of Denise's prior history, care, and treatments so they could use that for her file and not waste our time having to explain it to them during one of our limited appointments. The letter also challenged the doctor. It stated that if he was interested only in simple cases of bacteria and viruses then this was not the case for him. But, if he was up for a challenge and wanted to attempt to accomplish something great then this would be a case of great interest to him. I also spelled out my conditions of being the patient advocate and the contact person for Denise. That I was demanding and could even be considered a royal pain from time to time. I told them that I was not interested in wasting their time but only in making sure that Denise was well taken care of. I held nothing back, as I never wanted to have to go through anything like what had just occurred again.

First, I sent the e-mail to Witt Curry, Dan's family physician. Witt was quick to respond to my e-mail and letter and said he was not the man for the job. He said he was semi-retired and felt the case would be too demanding due to his lack of time. I appreciated his honesty. He did, however, recommend a young doctor named Dan Rubin who had just completed his residency and did have the time to dedicate to our case. He said that he had discussed it with Dr. Rubin and shared my letter with him and that Dr. Rubin was very interested in the case. He stated that I should call him if I wanted to discuss it with him further.

I called Dr. Rubin, and we set up an appointment. We met, and he was extremely helpful and was glad to allow me to help in solving the problem with Denise's liver situation. I told him that I suspected the Dylantin was the culprit, and after consulting information from his palm pilot, he agreed that Phenitoin was toxic to the liver over time, and it would make perfect sense to take her off the Dylantin and check her levels again in two weeks. The only problem was that we did not want to leave susceptible to a seizure, so we would have to come up with an alternative drug that was not absorbed by the liver.

He wrote down the names of three drugs and asked me to research them and see which one I thought would be best. Then, he said he would consult some neurologists that he knew, and we would discuss our findings together. This was the first time a doctor put any confidence in me, and my ego was quite happy. A couple of days later he called me and asked me what I had found. I told him that one of the drugs was related to several deaths and another actually was toxic to the liver. The third drug, Neurontin looked the most promising to me and that would be my drug of choice. He actually agreed and said that was what he recommended! We took Denise of the Dylantin immediately and replaced it with a moderate dose of the Neurontin.

Two weeks later a blood test was performed and her liver enzymes had returned to the normal range! I couldn't believe how simple that was and that it had taken over three months to get to the bottom of the problem, unbelievable. Dr. Rubin was my hero.

Sadly, on her next MRI four new lesions were discovered. It confirmed to me, at least in my mind, that the therapy Denise had been on was probably working before it was taken away. We treated the tumors with radiation, as we had done in the past, and Denise was put back on the therapy. However, she would never experience a reprieve as long as she had before these latest lesions were found, and we would never know what could have been.

A Place to Rest

But if I had another minute,
I'd put my arms around my baby
and I'd hold her like I'd never done before.
I'd tell her not to worry,
I'd tell her I'd be waiting
when her turn came to knock on heaven's door.
But then again, I might decide to fall down on my
knees
and thank God for the life I've loved so dear.
I'd ask Him to send peace to each of us,
as long as we are here
that's if I had another minute.
David M. Bailey, "If I Had Another"[22]

The following Friday, November 12, 2004, a memorial service was held at the First Baptist Church of Naples. There
was a tremendous turnout, and a beautiful service was offi-
ciated by Pastor Hayes Wicker. We thought it would be
nice to hold services in both Naples and in Gainesville so
that all who loved Denise would have an opportunity to
say goodbye to their faithful friend, Denise. Therefore, two
days later, we held a second memorial service at Trinity
United Methodist Church in Gainesville. There were prob-

ably three to four hundred people there to attend what we referred to as a "Celebration Service" to celebrate the life of Denise. Attending both of these services took a lot out of me, but I really wanted to honor Denise and share those final moments of reflection with all of our wonderful friends and family members.

Denise had inspired so many with her bright light of enthusiasm and encouragement. Ironically, many friends were made with people who were interested in helping Denise in one way or another, but in many ways, it would be Denise who helped them instead. Denise had this amazing ability to find people searching for hope, and Denise, with God's help, always showed them that there was always hope available, no matter how desperate your situation is. The service we held at Trinity was a good example of how Denise lived her life. Her service was upbeat and positive. Ed Garvin and his band WSU (short for Whoever Shows Up), played inspiring Hymns such as, "Shall We Gather at the River," "Will the Circle Be Unbroken," "This Little Light of Mine," and the "Hymn of Promise."

The music was played in an up-tempo, and as I stood up and clapped my hands to the music, the other three to four hundred observers did the same. We were determined to "celebrate" on this, the saddest of days. We had all lost something that was extremely special that could never, ever be replaced. However, we were all very fortunate to have known and shared all the special moments with Denise and we knew it. I felt most fortunate of all because she had been my wife, and it was an honor for me to have been her husband.

What was written on the back of the service program spoke volumes about the person Denise was.

> Denise was so *Encouraging*—always positive, always smiling. Denise's oncologist referred to her as a "Radiant Candle and the reason why I practice medicine." She was and will remain as the light of my life. Jesus said it like this in Luke 11:33–36,
>
>> No one lights a lamp and puts it in a place where it will be hidden, or under a bowl. Instead he puts it on its stand, so that those who come in may see the light. Your eye is the lamp of your body. When your eyes are good, your whole body also is full of light. But when they are bad, your body also is full of darkness. See to it, then that the light within you is not darkness. Therefore, if your whole body is full of light, and no part of it dark, it will be completely lighted, as when the light of a lamp shines on you.
>
> Denise's light will never fade. Like sparklers on the Fourth of July, her light will continuously be passed on from one person to another.

When the week was over, I was completely exhausted, physically and emotionally. Closure would not come for some time because Denise's final wishes were for her ashes to be left on the property of Trinity United Methodist Church, in Gainesville. Coincidentally, the church had been planning to create a garden on the property specifically for this purpose called the Trinity United Methodist Church Memorial Gardens. It would turn out to be a beautiful spot for people to leave their ashes. The trouble was that the gardens would not be ready until spring, so I waited until our pastor, Dan Johnson, gave me the go ahead to come up and complete the task. The last thing I wanted to do was to put my children and myself through another service, so the occasion was kept quiet until the day I decided to make the trip. I felt that once this was completed, Denise's friends could come, visit, and remember her as they wished

Sometime after Thanksgiving that year, I decided to take Raechel and Richard to Boone, North Carolina, to escape the sadness over the Christmas holidays. The kids had never seen snow, and so I thought there was nothing like an early snowstorm to take our minds off everything. My sister Donna warned that in Boone, before Christmas, it could be as warm as sixty degrees and no snow on the ground. However, I truly felt like God was going to provide us with a small blizzard, and he did not disappoint us. We had a ball! On the final leg of our journey to Boone, the skies opened up with a blizzard of beautiful snow, and we pulled off the road and enjoyed our first ever snowball fight! Raechel, Richard, and I were celebrating the truth of God's promise to us by making snowballs and pelting each other with them as fast as we could make them!

On one day, I took the kids snow skiing for the first time, and it was then, on my way up the hill on the chair lift, that I felt relief for the first time. As I was riding up the hill looking at the gorgeous surroundings, I felt as if a tremendous burden was lifted off my shoulders and I had something to look forward to for the first time in almost ten years. Denise had been taken from us and the fight was over. And most importantly, Denise was no longer suffering and enduring treatment after painful treatment. *Oh how she had suffered.* Now, we felt assured she was in a much, much better place than she was before. Perhaps now I could look forward to moving on with my life, finish the task of raising our children and perhaps enjoy life without the dark cloud that had been over me for so long. I was ready to begin a new life with a fresh start. It was such a good yet unfamiliar feeling, and hard to describe.

Conclusion

Nothing I can do nothing I can say.
Can make you love me more,
Your love remains the same.
You gave it all for me,
You gladly took my place.
To rid myself of all, all my guilt and shame
I must have stood strong, I must have stood tight
To yield the thoughts around me,
The battle in my mind
And knowing you surround me,
Your wings coat my despair.
Whatever my condition,
The cross it shows you care"
Jeremy Camp, "Nothing" [23]

I loved my wife, Denise, with all of my heart, body, and soul!
I tried desperately to keep Denise alive and would have given
my own life for her if only I could have. In the twelve plus
years that we were together, I never, ever considered being
with anyone other than her. We were made to be together,
and we were perfect for each other. Unfortunately, God took
her away from me, and there was nothing I could do about it

in the end. And as the saying goes ... "The good Lord giveth and the good Lord taketh away."

I began writing this book back in December of 2004 while vacationing in the snow with Raechel and Richard. Almost two years have gone by now and I am finally putting the final words in writing. I have to ask myself, *what is it I want you to get out of this story?* The first thing I want you to know is what an exceptional person Denise Ellis was. I have never in my life met anyone with half of the zest for life that she had. She was courageous, strong, determined, faithful, positive, and committed. She was an incredible mother to her two children; you don't have to know Denise to know that, all you have to do is to meet either of her children. She was a loving and faithful wife, whom I miss dearly and will always remember. I am so thankful that she was my wife for twelve difficult yet wonderful years, and I was privileged to help her through her ordeal. She was an incredible friend to all those who met her, and it has been said that she never met a stranger. Most importantly, she was as good an example of what a follower of Christ should be.

Secondly, I could never say enough nice things about the friends we made and the people who gave of themselves to help us. The people of Trinity UMC, Capri Christian Church, and First Baptist Church of Naples were amazing. All of my family, friends, and people that I work with at Cracklin' Jacks who were so supportive, you are the best, thank you! There is no question that God was working through each and every one of you for his greater purpose. I did not deserve your kindness and generosity, but you gave it to me just the same.

Lastly, I would implore you to do all you can to put your faith in God, more specifically, Jesus Christ. Our experience taught us to put our priorities in order and how to really live life. We spent our time with our children, family, and friends, and we were rewarded for it. I gave up many of the selfish things I liked to do for myself and instead invested in God and family and life is good. Money, travel, and material things are way over-rated and will be gone in a short time. Investing in relationships with Jesus, family, and friends lasts forever.

I want you to know that I am just a simple man who was blind when this story began but observed and recognized all that God was doing and could no longer deny his existence. And I think it is important for you to remember that this story didn't have a rosy ending. Denise and I never found a cure, and she was eventually taken away from my children and me. She was only thirty-five years old when she died. God did not give us all that we asked for, but we are still thankful for all he did, and we love him for it.

I will end this story the same as it began, sitting and talking with my good friend Ed Garvin. I sent Ed an advanced copy of this story a few weeks ago and asked him to read it and give me any feedback he might have. Fortunately, I spent a few days in Ormond Beach a few days before Christmas, and it just so happened that Ed and his family were doing the same a few miles north in my favorite city, St. Augustine. So there were Ed and I, sitting on the porch of his beach-house rental and Ed asked me, "So, Rod, tell me, what do you think your book is about?"

"Well Ed," I answered, "It is about all that Denise and I went through and how God really and truly came to our aid."

Ed then said, "I don't mean this in a bad way, Rod, but I think the book is about you and all that you went through and how you dealt with your situation as an advocate for Denise."

"I suppose that is true," I responded, "But I had hoped that this book would be a way of honoring God and Denise, at the same time. That perhaps people would read it and realize that God is real and that He truly exists and takes action on our behalf." Ed did not necessarily disagree with that, but his point was that perhaps this book would be most useful to someone who was going through what I had gone through. Perhaps other caregivers would benefit most from reading this book. I realized that the truth is, we are all caregivers, and we are the caregivers to our very own souls. This book is written for the caregivers in each and every one of us so that our souls may be saved.

The truth is Ed is right. This book is about me and what happened to me. That is my point—it is a true account of what actually occurred. If that is true then isn't God truly amazing and don't you think it is time to turn to him? My hope is that anyone who reads this will be helped or inspired by what has occurred in some meaningful way. But mostly, I hope that at least one person, who had little or no faith, will read this text and will be able to take just one small step into their faith. Perhaps that will be the step that leads them into a deep and continuous relationship with Jesus.

There are plenty of books out there that talk about faith that discuss ideas and feelings and all sorts of wonderful thoughts about God, but how many of them list occurrence after occurrence of just what God did to show himself to us? Denise knew what God was doing for her, and she would want you to know what he can and will do for you. God is real, and he puts meaning into life and takes the sting out of death. All we have to do is believe. What else can I do? What else can I say? Life is short and can prove to be very difficult so don't delay! Trust him, and you will not be sorry! Blessed be the name of the Lord.

Endnotes

1. Owens, Ginney, "If You Want Me To," *Without Condition* (Rocketown Records, 1999)

2. Jars of Clay, "Trouble Is," *Who We Are Instead* (Brentwood Records, 2003)

3. FFH, "Open Up The Sky," *Far From Home* (Essential Records, 2007)

4. Chesney, Kenny, "Me And You," *Me And You* (Bna Entertainment, 1996)

5. *The Exorcist*, directed by William Friedkin, (Warner Bros., 1973)

6. Jars of Clay, "Much Afraid," *Much Afraid* (Silvertone Records, 1997)

7. Jars of Clay, "Worlds Apart," *Jars of Clay* (Silvertone Records, 1995)

8. Brown, Jackson, "I'll Do Anything," *I'm Alive* (Elektra Records, 1993)

9. Brown, Jackson, "I'll Do Anything," *I'm Alive* (Elektra Records, 1993))

10. Knapp, Jennifer, "Hold Me Now," *Collection* (Gotee Records 2004)

11. National Cancer Institute, "U.S. National Institutes of Health," http://www.cancer.gov (accessed November 8, 2007).

12. Third Day, "40 Days," *Come Together* (Essential Records, 2001)

13. Jars of Clay, "Faith Enough," *Who We Are Instead* (Brentwood Records, 2003)

14. Bailey, David M., "Hey," *Life* (CD Baby Records, 2000)

15. *Gladiator*, directed by Ridley Scott, (Dreamworks, 2000)

16. Third Day, "Show Me Your Glory," *Come Together* (Essential Records, 2001)

17. Third Day, "Can't Stop The Rain," *Come Together* (Essential Records, 2001)

18. Jefferson, "KimmelCancerCenter," http://www.kimmel-cancercenter.org/kcc/kccnew/clinicalcare/cancerclinical-trials/getprotocols.php?PrimarySite=melanoma (accessed November 12, 2007).

19. Knapp, Jennifer, "Martyrs And Thieves," *Kansas* (Gotee Records, 1998)

20. Tree 63, "Blessed Be Your Name," *Answer To The Question* (Inpop Records 2004)

21. *Merriam-Webster's Online Dictionary*, s.v. "enemy," http://www.merriam-webster.com/dictionary/enemy (accessed November 12, 2007).

22. Bailey, David M., "If I Had Another," *Life* (CD Baby Records, 2000)

23. Camp, Jeremy, "Nothing," *Stay* (BEC Recordings, 2002)